ONE POT FAVOURITES

Pete Evans

This book is dedicated to everyone who loves to fill their home with intoxicating aromas, to excite their tastebuds with delicious flavours and, most importantly, to nourish their body with the most effective form of medicine on the planet — beautiful and nutritious food, cooked from the heart, always with love and laughter.

ONE POT FAVOURITES

Pete Evans

plum. Pan Macmillan Australia

CONTENTS

INTRODUCTION

G'day everyone. Thank you for taking the time to read and cook from this book. I am so proud of the wonder-filled pages and recipes contained here! I'm also excited about adding some amazing new dishes to your cooking repertoire – ones that the whole family will love.

One pot cooking is something that each and every culture around the world has done since our ancestors learnt how to cook with fire hundreds of thousands of years ago. While I am a huge fan of eating raw vegetable, seafood and meat dishes – especially in summer when I crave light, fresh food – as soon as the weather becomes a bit cooler, I start to think about warm, comforting dishes to nourish me. Dishes that have a little more fat and that are often cooked in a bone broth. And this desire for more hearty dishes that can be prepared simply in one cooking vessel is what led me to create this book.

All of the delicious one pot meals in this book are paleo inspired, as this way of eating provides our body with the right kind of fuel to perform at its best. When you follow this kind of lifestyle, you are allowing your body to thrive on the foods we have evolved to eat. Paleo embraces real foods and eliminates foods that may cause inflammation in our bodies. The most common culprits for this are gluten (and grains), legumes, dairy, toxic oils (such as seed and vegetable oils) and refined sugars. If you have an autoimmune issue, you may also consider eliminating nightshade vegetables (such as tomatoes, eggplants, capsicums and potatoes), nuts and eggs for a period of time, too, to see how that impacts your health.

So what foods do we embrace? You'll be pleased to know that there is an abundance of natural and delicious food to include in your diet. Here are our recommendations:

* Eat up to a palm-sized portion of animal protein at every meal. Focus on sourcing protein from animals that have had a natural diet, such as grass-fed beef, wild-caught seafood, free-range and pasture-raised poultry and pigs, and wild game.

* Enjoy an abundance of organic vegetables, with a preference for the least starchy varieties.

* Include good-quality fat from avocados, olives, nuts, seeds, eggs and animals in your daily diet.

* Include bone broth in your daily diet for good gut health. You can drink bone broth straight up, or add it to soups, curries or braises.

* Add a spoon of fermented vegetables to every meal if possible. Start off with a teaspoon a day, then work your way up to about a tablespoon or two per meal. Always serve fermented veg cold, as heating it will destroy the beneficial bacteria.

As with any dietary changes, always consult your health professional and inform them of your intentions to make sure they feel it is safe for you, taking into account your overall health and any medical conditions that you may have. Luckily, more and more doctors are promoting this way of life for their patients, which is wonderful to see.

In the coming pages, I hope to give you loads of ideas for one pot meals, whether you're using a saucepan, casserole dish, tagine, cast iron pot, wok or even a roasting tin. Many recipes also include instructions for using your slow cooker or pressure cooker. Slow cookers are brilliant for cooking cheaper cuts of meat until they are meltingly tender and are a great way to make sure that dinner is ready when you get home – simply get the meal started in the morning before work and it should be ready at the end of the day. I also love to pop the slow cooker on before I go to bed, so that there's a beautiful and hearty meal waiting for me at breakfast time. Pressure cookers work quite differently to slow cookers, but they are another fabulous time-saving device in the kitchen. Cooking your meal at high pressure means that everything is ready much quicker. For more information on using slow cookers and pressure cookers, see pages 11–13.

I have tried to include many family favourites to keep everyone happy – there are some exciting new versions of the classic roast chicken, kid-friendly curries and wholesome stews. However, I have also included some more challenging recipes that include different types of offal to encourage you to step out of your comfort zone. I know that many people feel unsure of cooking and eating offal, but I urge you to at least give it a try, as it's incredibly nutritious and also pretty damn flavoursome.

Before you get started on your one pot adventure, I have a few tips and tricks to help you on your way:

* Double or triple these recipes so that you can have leftovers for days or freeze for later. Just be careful not to overfill your pot – use two if necessary.

* Get your partner or family involved in cooking by setting them the challenge of cooking one dish a week from this book for a year. If that's too much, ask them to at least help out in the kitchen – we all know that many hands make light work!

* Play around with different proteins in these recipes. If lamb shank doesn't fit your budget or isn't available, swap it for gravy beef or chicken thighs. If a curry recipe calls for liver but you are not keen on it, simply replace it with some good-quality animal protein of your choice (and alter the cooking time to suit).

* Serve these dishes with a side of vegetables or salad (unless the dish has a lot of veggies already) and have some fermented vegetables on the side for good gut health.

* Always use your own homemade broths rather than store-bought varieties, which are usually full of salt and other additives. If you don't have any homemade broth, simply use water instead.

* Try to be prepared so that you have enough time to cook these recipes. Make a meal plan for the week ahead and do your shopping on the weekend to make weeknights a little easier.

* If you have the space, think about investing in a large chest freezer so that you can buy your meat in bulk. Lots of people are now buying half a cow or a whole lamb direct from farmers. This is a great way to save money as well as support farmers who are passionate about the health of their animals.

So, that's enough from me, it's time to get stuck into the cooking. As always, I believe the most important thing is to cook with love and laughter. I love to put on my favourite music and have fun when I spend time in the kitchen with my partner, Nic, and my two daughters, Chilli and Indii. Savour this time with your family and make it a special part of your daily routine. There is nothing more enjoyable and satisfying than preparing nutritious food for yourself and your loved ones.

ONE POT BASICS

Getting Started

When it comes to dinnertime, most of us would love a beautiful home-cooked meal on the table every night, but we are all so busy these days that it can seem hard to achieve. And that's where one pot cooking comes in! Because the meals in this book can be cooked in just one casserole dish, saucepan, frying pan or wok, there isn't much hard work to be done at all, and there's hardly any mess to clean up. And you'll be surprised by the huge range of things you can make in a single cooking vessel – soups, stews, braises, casseroles, curries, roasts and stir-fries.

I like to get all of my ingredients and equipment ready on the bench before I start cooking, so that I'm not messing around looking in the back of the cupboard for these things once I get stuck into the recipe. While some one pot dishes can be made very quickly, many are cooked low and slow to achieve an incredible flavour. It's important to not hurry this cooking time, and to follow the recipes closely in regards to when to add each element, so that every part of the dish is cooked perfectly.

I've given some tips for one pot cooking below, as well as some more detailed instructions for using a pressure cooker or slow cooker. Really though, one pot cooking is about as simple as it gets, so there's not much more to do except get cooking some of these delicious recipes. Enjoy!

TIPS FOR ONE POT COOKING

* After you brown your meat, use the same pot to cook your onions and garlic, then add your meat back to the dish. This will help develop the flavours in your dish.

* Completely thaw your meat before cooking to ensure that it cooks evenly.

* Most of the dishes in this book have a long cooking time, so it's best to add soft herbs like parsley or coriander at the end of the cooking process to get the most flavour out of them.

* Before searing meat in the pan, ensure that the pan is very hot. This will caramelise your meat evenly without cooking it through too much. You just want a golden seal on all sides of the meat, as this will help put more flavour in your dishes.

Pressure Cookers

Pressure cookers have been around for centuries, and they are a fabulous way of getting dinner on the table in a flash. They use heat and steam to cook food really quickly, though they are not suitable for cooking every single kind of meal. You will see that throughout this book I have added pressure-cooking instructions for the tough cuts of meat, stews, curries, braises, soups and some vegetable dishes. All pressure cooker instructions in this book are for stovetop cookers. If you have an electric pressure cooker at home you will need to increase the cooking time (*see* Types of Pressure Cookers).

HOW TO USE YOUR PRESSURE COOKER

When using the pressure cooker instructions in this book you will notice the method says to bring the cooker to high pressure. This means turning the stovetop burner to high heat and then when the cooker reaches full pressure reducing the heat to medium. This will allow the pot to maintain pressure while cooking. You don't need to do this with an electric cooker, as it will automatically do this for you.

Pressure cookers need to generate a substantial amount of steam, so at least 1 cup of liquid is needed for them to work properly, but be careful not to use too much liquid. There are markings on the pressure cooker pot to indicate how far you can fill up the pressure cooker with liquid. It is important to have all the food in the pot first and then add the liquid, so you don't go over the advised marking. If your pot doesn't have markings, don't fill it more than half way with liquid and no more than two-thirds with food. And never pack the food tightly when adding it to your pressure cooker. If you don't follow these rules the pressure cooker may not work efficiently, which may affect the end result and can also cause the safety valve to activate.

NATURAL RELEASE VS QUICK RELEASE

Most pressure cooker recipes call for two methods of opening the pot and letting out the steam: natural release and quick release.

Natural release means just turning the heat off and letting the pressure cooker sit on the stovetop. The food will keep on cooking, but the internal temperature will drop from 120°C to 100°C, which makes it possible to safely open the lid. This process will take about 15 minutes. This natural release method will tenderise the meat more as the pressure drops, and I highly recommend using this method in most of my recipes.

Quick release means you can bring the pressure down fast by opening the valve that releases the steam. This method is helpful when you wish to add additional ingredients, such as vegetables, to the pressure cooker half way or at the end of the cooking process, or if you want to cook something very fast and you need to stop the cooking process quickly to prevent from overcooking, e.g. fish, offal, eggs and sausages. It's important not to use this method if you have a lot of liquid in the pressure cooker because when the valve is released it may spray out hot liquid or clog up the valve. Also avoid this method when cooking meat because the rapid release of pressure may cause the meat to toughen.

TYPES OF PRESSURE COOKERS

There are three types of pressure cookers on the market. First generation pressure cookers (stovetop) operate using a weight-modified valve, also called a jigger valve, that suddenly releases pressure and makes a whistle sound. With first generation pressure cookers it is possible to open the lid before the steam has escaped, so if you are using your granny's old pot be careful to release all the pressure before opening the lid to avoid a big mess or worse an injury.

Second generation pressure cookers (stovetop) are most commonly used today. Spring valves replace the weight valve and most don't release any steam, so in other words they are non-venting. You will have to manually release the pressure once your food is cooked or use the natural release method.

Third generation pressure cookers are electric, providing pre-programmed settings that can be controlled through digital displays. Electric pressure cookers require no monitoring of the pressure, but it does take a little longer than with a stovetop pressure cooker. (Cooking time for stovetop vs electric is 10 vs 13 minutes, and natural release is 15 vs 25 minutes.)

STAYING SAFE WHEN USING A PRESSURE COOKER

Safety is everything and it's very important to take extreme care when dealing with hot appliances, especially pressure cookers. Your pressure cooker generates a great amount of steam, which reaches up to 120ºC, so when releasing the valve take extreme care. Make sure you follow all of the manufacturer's instructions and carefully read the safety information for your pressure cooker before you use it.

TIPS FOR USING A PRESSURE COOKER

✳ Never ever force the lid open! Not only could you get seriously injured, you will also have to deal with a big mess. When opening the lid of the pressure cooker, always remove the lid by tilting it away from you to allow any excess steam to escape.

✳ Become familiar with the manufacturer's instructions before operating the device. Different models of pressure cooker have different parts and therefore different instructions.

✳ Read and understand the recipes before you begin cooking.

✳ It is best to brown the meat first to intensify the flavour. This can be done in the pressure cooker pot or in a frying pan.

✳ Food that is used in the pressure cooker should be uniform in size to make sure that it is all cooked evenly.

✳ Use a timer when using a pressure cooker. Start the timer when the pot reaches full pressure, at that stage you will need to reduce the heat to medium (see How to Use Your Pressure Cooker).

✳ When using a pressure cooker, very little liquid evaporates during the cooking process, so it's always best to reduce the amount of liquid in the original recipe by at least one-third. I have already measured this for you in the pressure cooker instructions in this book.

Slow Cookers

Slow cookers are perfect for busy families and individuals who are on the go. They are a wonderful way to create an incredibly flavoursome meal with very little effort.

The slow cooking method has been around for centuries, but the first electric slow cooker was introduced in the 1970s and was called the crock-pot. It became a huge trend the mid 70s, but when microwaves came out a few years later people started to zap their food instead and the slow cookers got left behind. However, slow cookers have made a comeback and people are embracing this style of cooking once more.

Slow cookers are fabulous for transforming tougher cuts of meats into a meltingly tender and delicious meal. They use very little electricity and there's only one dish used, so makes the washing up very easy.

Slow cookers are safe to walk away from and leave unattended, so you don't need to hover over it during the cooking process, just let it do the work. Also, there's no stirring involved.

When you're using the low setting, the food should be cooked for 8–10 hours, and if you're using the high setting, cooking time is usually 4–6 hours.

Slow cookers are usually covered with a lid that fits the pot nice and snuggly, so no steam can escape. The slow cooker works by bringing your food to a temperature between 95–150ºC, maintaining a stable heat throughout the process.

TIPS FOR USING A SLOW COOKER

✳ Always read the manufacturer's instructions before using your slow cooker, as models will vary slightly.

✳ Slow cookers are designed to do their own thing, so you don't need to keep checking and opening the lid. Each time you open the lid you will release some heat, and you will need to increase the cooking time.

✳ Because slow cookers only have 2 temperatures, you can't brown your meat or vegetables in the pot. It's best do this in a frying pan first, so you will get better flavours at the end.

✳ When slow cooking, not much liquid evaporates during the cooking process, so it's always best to reduce the amount of liquid in the original recipe by at least one-third. In the slow cooker instructions in this book, I have already measured this for you.

✳ Fill the slow cooker at least halfway to two-third full, nothing more or nothing less.

Borscht with macadamia cream
and dill * FRENCH ONION SOUP *
Spiced pumpkin soup * CAULIFLOWER
FRIED RICE WITH ASIAN GREENS
* Roasted turnip with fennel, lemon and chilli *
MOROCCAN VEGETABLE TAGINE
* Whole roasted cauliflower with almonds and
dukkah * SIMPLE BRAISED VEG * Thai
red vegetable curry * WILD MUSHROOM
'RISOTTO' WITH CHESTNUTS AND
TRUFFLE OIL * Creamy cauliflower
and coconut curry * SWEDE AND
SPINACH CURRY

Chapter One
VEGETABLES

If you have never made borscht, here's a real treat for you and your loved ones. This is definitely one of my favourite soups. I wonder if it has anything to do with all those marrow bones that are gently simmered in the soup to build a depth of flavour that is just so moreish? Delicious served with lovely seeded bread rolls and some whipped tallow and sea salt.

BORSCHT *with*

SERVES 4–6 ## MACADAMIA CREAM AND DILL

1 tablespoon coconut oil or
   good-quality animal fat*
½ onion, finely chopped
2 garlic cloves, finely chopped
1 kg bone marrow bones, cut into
   8 cm lengths, split in half
   (ask your butcher to do this)
1 bay leaf
2.5 litres Beef or Chicken Bone
   Broth (pages 230 and 234)
   or water
½ small white cabbage (about
   500 g), finely diced or coarsely
   grated
1 sweet potato (about 330 g), diced
1 carrot, diced
4 beetroot (about 300 g), diced
½ small celeriac (about 320 g),
   diced
½ small parsnip (about 75 g), diced
½ small turnip (about 75 g), diced
125 g canned diced tomatoes
   (or 125 g tomatoes, diced)
2½ tablespoons red wine vinegar
½ teaspoon coconut sugar
dill fronds, to serve

Macadamia cream
160 g (1 cup) macadamia nuts,
   soaked in 750 ml water for
   8 hours or overnight
juice of 1 lemon

* See Glossary

❶ For the macadamia cream, drain the nuts, rinse and drain again. Transfer to a food processor and pulse to finely chop. Add the lemon juice and 100 ml water and process until smooth, adding extra water or lemon juice to thin if necessary.

❷ Melt the oil or fat in a large saucepan over low heat, add the onion and garlic and sauté for 3–4 minutes until soft and just translucent.

❸ Place the marrow in the pan, add the bay leaf and broth or water and bring to the boil over medium heat. Simmer, skimming occasionally, for 30–40 minutes until reduced to about 2 litres. Remove the bones and scrape any marrow into the broth.

❹ Increase the heat to high. Add the cabbage to the pan, bring to the boil, then add the sweet potato and carrot.

❺ Reduce the heat to low and simmer, half-covered with a lid, until the vegetables are just tender, 30–40 minutes.

❻ Add the remaining ingredients, except the dill, to the pan.

❼ Half-cover the pan with the lid and simmer (do not boil) for 50 minutes–1 hour until the vegetables are very tender. Thin the soup with extra water if necessary.

❽ Ladle the soup into bowls, top with the macadamia cream and dill and serve.

PRESSURE COOKER Don't overfill your pressure cooker – you may need to halve this recipe. Follow step ❶. Follow step ❷, using your pressure cooker over high heat. Reduce heat to medium–high and follow step ❸. Follow step ❹, close the lid and lock it, then bring to high pressure. Reduce heat to medium and cook for 10 minutes. Let the pressure drop for 2 minutes before using the quick release method to open (see page 11). Follow step ❻, close and lock the lid, then bring to high pressure and cook for 10 minutes. Let the pressure drop naturally before opening the lid. Follow step ❽.

SLOW COOKER Follow steps ❶–❷. Follow step ❸, then transfer the cooked vegetables, marrow bones, bay leaf and broth or water to your slow cooker. Cover and cook on high for 2½ hours. Add the cabbage, sweet potato and carrot, cover and cook on low for 6 hours. Follow step ❻, cover and cook for 3 hours on low. Follow step ❽.

How can anyone say no to a French onion soup that is full of delicious gut-healing beef broth, health-giving onion (known for regulating blood sugar) and medicinal garlic and thyme? Enjoy this when you want a nourishing breakfast, lunch or dinner. If you are looking for a more hearty dish, add some bone marrow, braised short ribs or beef cheek.

French ONION SOUP

SERVES 4–6

2 tablespoons coconut oil or good-quality animal fat*

1.5 kg onions, sliced

4 garlic cloves, chopped

2 teaspoons finely chopped thyme leaves

1.5 litres (6 cups) Beef or Chicken Bone Broth (pages 230 and 234) or vegetable stock

2 bay leaves

sea salt and freshly ground black pepper

2 macadamia nuts (activated if possible*), finely grated, to serve

a few slices of paleo bread, to serve

* See Glossary

❶ Melt the oil or fat in a large, heavy-based saucepan over medium–high heat. Add the onion and cook, stirring occasionally, for 30 minutes until the onion is soft and beginning to brown.

❷ Add the garlic and thyme, reduce the heat to medium–low and cook, stirring occasionally, for 30 minutes until the onion is caramelised.

❸ Increase the heat to medium and, stirring constantly, gradually pour in the broth or stock, then add the bay leaves.

❹ Bring to the boil, skimming off any scum that rises to the surface. Reduce the heat to low and simmer gently for 50 minutes until the soup is full of flavour with a nicely balanced sweetness. Season with salt and pepper.

❺ Ladle the soup into bowls, sprinkle some grated macadamia over the top and serve with some paleo bread on the side.

PRESSURE COOKER Follow step ❶ using your pressure cooker over medium–high heat. Follow step ❷ using your pressure cooker over medium heat. Follow step ❸, close the lid and lock it, then bring the cooker to high pressure, reduce the heat to medium to maintain pressure and cook for 15 minutes. Let the pressure drop naturally before opening the lid. Follow step ❺.

SLOW COOKER Follow steps ❶–❷, then transfer the onion mixture to your slow cooker. Follow step ❸, cover and cook on low for 6–8 hours Follow step ❺.

Note If you like a slightly thicker soup, you can add 1–2 teaspoons of tapioca flour when you add the broth or stock.

Who doesn't love a bowl of luscious, lightly spiced pumpkin soup on a cold winter's night? Pumpkin soup tends to tick a lot of boxes for families – it is super cheap, nutritious, pleasing to all tastebuds and perfect for leftovers the next day. Try packing it as a school lunch in a thermos, or enjoying it for a quick breakfast with a poached egg or some leftover roasted chicken, pork or lamb on top.

Spiced PUMPKIN SOUP

3 tablespoons coconut oil or good-quality animal fat*

1 kg butternut pumpkin (or any other pumpkin variety), peeled and diced

1 carrot, diced

1 large onion, finely chopped

4 garlic cloves, crushed

1.3 litres Chicken Bone Broth (page 234) or vegetable stock

1½ tablespoons finely grated ginger

1½ tablespoons ras el hanout (see note)

1½ teaspoons ground cumin

6 saffron threads

1 teaspoon dried chilli flakes (optional)

250 ml (1 cup) coconut cream, plus extra to serve

sea salt and freshly ground black pepper

coriander and mint leaves, to serve

chilli powder, to serve

See Glossary

❶ Melt the oil or fat in a large saucepan over medium heat. Add the pumpkin, carrot, onion and garlic and sauté, stirring occasionally, for about 10 minutes, until the onion is translucent.

❷ Add the broth or stock, ginger, ras el hanout, cumin, saffron and chilli flakes (if using). Reduce the heat, cover and simmer, stirring occasionally, for about 30 minutes, or until the carrot and pumpkin are tender. Add the coconut cream and puree the soup using a hand-held blender. Season with salt and pepper.

❸ Ladle the soup into bowls, drizzle with a little extra coconut cream and top with some coriander and mint leaves and chilli powder.

Note Ras el hanout is a North African spice mix that consists of over 12 spices. I like to use Herbie's Spices' ras el hanout in this recipe.

On a busy weeknight, I love a one-wok number that we can whip up and pop on the table in less than 20 minutes. And here is just the thing. If you want to serve this as a main meal and you feel like adding a little animal protein, some good choices are prawns, crabmeat, chicken and bacon. Alternatively, simply serve on the side with a grilled piece of fish or some lamb chops rubbed with Chinese five spice.

Cauliflower FRIED RICE

SERVES 4–6 WITH ASIAN GREENS

1 head of cauliflower (about 800 g), separated into florets
4 eggs
sea salt and freshly ground white pepper
2½ tablespoons coconut oil
½ onion, finely chopped
2 garlic cloves, finely chopped
150 g shiitake or oyster mushrooms (or a mixture of both), sliced
2.5 cm piece of ginger, finely grated
100 g okra*, sliced
250 g bok choy, shredded
100 g Chinese broccoli (gai larn), chopped
2 tablespoons tamari or coconut aminos*
3 tablespoons Chicken Bone Broth (page 234) or water
50 g bean sprouts
2 spring onions, finely sliced
2 tablespoons each chopped flat-leaf parsley and coriander leaves
1 large handful of water spinach or baby spinach, roughly chopped

To serve
coriander leaves
toasted sesame seeds
fish sauce
lime wedges
1 long red chilli, finely sliced

* See Glossary

❶ Place the cauliflower in the bowl of a food processor and pulse until it resembles rice.

❷ Whisk the eggs with a little salt and pepper. Place a large frying pan or wok over high heat and add ½ tablespoon of the oil. Pour in the egg and tilt the pan so that it covers the base. Cook for a couple of minutes, or until the egg is set. Remove from the pan, slice into thick strips and set aside.

❸ Heat the remaining oil in the pan over medium–high heat, add the onion and garlic and cook for a few minutes until soft. Stir in the mushrooms and ginger and cook for another few minutes until softened slightly. Add the okra, bok choy and Chinese broccoli and cook for 2 minutes. Stir in the cauliflower rice and cook for 2–3 minutes until tender.

❹ Return the egg to the pan and add the tamari or coconut aminos, broth or water, sprouts, spring onion, herbs, spinach and some salt and pepper and cook for 1–2 minutes until everything is heated through and well combined.

❺ Serve with some coriander and sesame seeds and a splash of fish sauce, a squeeze of lime and a sprinkle of chilli.

I love roasting seasonal vegetables while I prepare a simple main course to accompany them. The meal might be as simple as serving spice-rubbed lamb chops, crackling chicken or grilled fish with a lovely bowl of these veggies and some aioli. Always make extras as these are delicious the next day to take to work or school for lunch.

Roasted TURNIP
SERVES 2 WITH FENNEL, LEMON AND CHILLI

4 tablespoons coconut oil or good-quality animal fat*, melted

1 onion, cut into wedges

4 turnips or swedes, cut into wedges

6 baby fennel bulbs, quartered, fronds reserved (or 1 large one, cut into 2.5 cm wedges)

1 garlic bulb, skin on, broken into cloves

¼ lemon, cut into thin wedges

1–2 long red chillies, deseeded and finely chopped

500 ml (2 cups) Chicken Bone Broth (page 234)

sea salt and freshly ground black pepper

* See Glossary

❶ Preheat the oven to 180ºC.

❷ Pour the oil or fat into a large roasting tin, scatter on the onion, turnip or swede, fennel, garlic, lemon and chilli in a single layer. Pour in the broth and season the vegetables with salt and pepper.

❸ Roast in the oven, stirring occasionally, for 1 hour, or until tender and golden.

❹ Scatter over the reserved fennel fronds and serve hot.

The tantalising flavours of Morocco are easy to replicate at home with this delicious vegetable tagine. This alone is enough for dinner, but you might like to add in some prawns, chicken or fish pieces right at the end so you don't overcook them. If you don't have harissa on hand, just add a little sprinkle of chilli flakes for some heat. Serve with fermented vegetables on the side.

SERVES 4

Moroccan Vegetable TAGINE

2 tablespoons coconut oil or good-
    quality animal fat*
1 red onion, chopped
4 garlic cloves, chopped
1 teaspoon finely grated ginger
2 teaspoons ground cumin
¼ teaspoon ground cinnamon
1 teaspoon ground turmeric
1 teaspoon paprika
1 pinch of saffron (about 15 threads)
1 tablespoon tomato paste
1 teaspoon harissa (optional)
300 g tomatoes, roughly chopped
300 g sweet potato, cut into 2 cm
    pieces
150 g parsnip, cut into 2 cm pieces
1 large carrot, cut into 2 cm pieces
100 g dates, pitted and chopped
100 g green olives, pitted
900 ml Chicken Bone Broth
    (page 234) or water
200 g fresh or frozen okra*
200 g broccoli, broken into florets
200 g cauliflower, broken into florets
2 zucchini (about 200 g), cut into
    2 cm pieces
sea salt and freshly ground
    black pepper
lemon wedges, to serve (optional)
coriander leaves, to serve
coconut yoghurt (for a recipe, see
    page 235), to serve

*See Glossary

❶ Melt the oil or fat in a large saucepan or tagine over medium heat. Add the onion and sauté for 5 minutes until soft. Add the garlic and ginger and cook for a further 30 seconds, then stir in the dried spices and sauté for 30 seconds until fragrant. Add the tomato paste and harissa (if using) and cook for 30 seconds, then add the tomato, sweet potato, parsnip, carrot, dates and olives and stir to combine. Pour in the broth or water, mix well and bring to the boil.

❷ Reduce the heat to low, cover the pan and simmer for 30 minutes until the vegetables are just tender.

❸ Add the okra, broccoli, cauliflower and zucchini to the pan.

❹ Cover the pan and cook for 15 minutes until all the vegetables are soft. Season with salt and pepper.

❺ To finish, serve directly from the pan or tagine or transfer to a large serving bowl. Squeeze over the lemon wedges (if using), sprinkle with the coriander leaves and serve with some coconut yoghurt.

PRESSURE COOKER Follow step ❶ using your pressure cooker, but add only 630 ml of broth or water rather than 900 ml. Close the lid and lock it, then bring the cooker to high pressure over high heat. Reduce the heat to medium to maintain pressure and cook for 3 minutes. Let the pressure drop naturally before opening the lid. Follow step ❸, then close and lock the lid. Bring the cooker to high pressure over high heat, then reduce heat to medium and cook for 4 minutes. Let the pressure drop naturally before opening the lid. Follow step ❺.

SLOW COOKER Follow step ❶, but add only 630 ml of broth or water rather than 900 ml. Transfer the vegetable mixture to your slow cooker. Cover and cook on high for 1½ hours, or until the vegetables are just soft. Follow step ❸, cover and cook on high for 1 hour, or until the vegetables are tender. Follow step ❺.

'Wow' is all I need to say about this dish! The process of roasting a whole cauliflower is amazing and here is my Middle Eastern take on it. Feel free to be inspired by other cuisines and flavour the cauliflower with your favourite herbs and spices.

Whole ROASTED *Cauliflower*
WITH ALMONDS AND DUKKAH
SERVES 4–6

1 large head of cauliflower
(about 800 g)
3 tablespoons coconut oil or good-quality animal fat*
2 onions, finely chopped
5 garlic cloves, finely sliced
1½ teaspoons ground turmeric
2 teaspoons cumin seeds
1 × 400 g can diced tomatoes
(or 400 g tomatoes, diced)
2 pinches of saffron
500 ml (2 cups) Beef or Chicken Bone Broth (pages 230 and 234) or water
sea salt and freshly ground black pepper
100 g almonds (activated if possible*), toasted and chopped
120 g dukkah (for a recipe, see page 236)
½ bunch of kale, silverbeet or spinach (about 200 g), stalks removed, leaves torn (reserve the stalks for broths)

* See Glossary

❶ Preheat the oven to 180°C.

❷ Remove the leaves and cut away the stalk from the base of the cauliflower.

❸ Melt the oil or fat in a large flameproof casserole dish that will fit your whole cauliflower. Add the onion and cook over medium heat for 5 minutes until soft. Stir in the garlic and cook for 1 minute, then add the turmeric and cumin seeds and cook for 30 seconds until fragrant.

❹ Add the tomatoes, saffron and broth or water to the dish, stir and bring to the boil. Remove from the heat and season with salt and pepper.

❺ Place the cauliflower in the dish and spoon the sauce over the top. Cover with foil and roast, basting every 20 minutes with the sauce, for 1–1½ hours until tender. Add a little more broth or water if it starts to look dry. Remove from the oven and set aside to cool a little.

❻ Combine the almonds and dukkah and mix well.

❼ When the cauliflower is cool enough to touch, coat it with the dukkah mixture, pressing it in with your hands to form an even crust. Scatter the kale over the sauce and mix through. Return to the oven and roast, uncovered, for a further 8–10 minutes until the cauliflower crust is golden brown.

We all sometimes face the dilemma of what to do with leftover vegetables in the bottom of the fridge. Well, you need never worry again, as you can simply braise them until tender in a little bone broth. They are the perfect accompaniment to a sensational roast. And for a delicious lunch, simply chill them and add some mayo, fresh herbs, animal protein (such as chicken, tuna or salmon) and fermented veg.

SERVES 4

Simple BRAISED VEG

2 tablespoons coconut oil or
    good-quality animal fat*
1 onion, cut into 1 cm thick wedges
3 garlic cloves, finely sliced
10 Dutch carrots, leafy tips trimmed
6 radishes, halved
3 turnips, cut into 3 cm pieces
¼ savoy cabbage, roughly chopped
1 green apple, cored and cut into
    2.5 cm pieces
250 ml (1 cup) Chicken Bone Broth
    (page 234) or water
2 bay leaves
sea salt and freshly ground
    black pepper

* See Glossary

❶ Preheat the oven to 180°C.

❷ Melt the oil or fat in a large flameproof casserole dish over medium heat. Add the onion and garlic and cook for 2 minutes until starting to colour slightly.

❸ Add the carrots, radish, turnip, cabbage and apple and cook, stirring occasionally, for 6 minutes until just starting to colour.

❹ Pour in the broth or water, add the bay leaves and season with salt and pepper.

❺ Cover with a lid or some foil and braise in the oven for 30 minutes until the vegetables are tender.

❻ Transfer the braised vegetables to a serving dish and serve.

PRESSURE COOKER Follow steps ❷–❸, using your pressure cooker over medium heat. Follow step ❹, close the lid and lock it, then bring the cooker to high pressure and cook over medium heat to maintain pressure for 5 minutes. Let the pressure drop naturally before opening the lid. Follow step ❻.

SLOW COOKER Follow steps ❷–❸, then transfer everything in the casserole dish to your slow cooker. Follow step ❹, cover and cook on low for 6 hours until the vegetables are cooked through. Follow step ❻.

I have to say the Thais do sensational and warming curries extremely well. Here a red curry paste is used as the base. You can make your own or there are some great organic ones available at good delis and markets that will save you time in the kitchen. If you want to include extra protein in your curry, add some chicken, lamb, pork, duck, beef or seafood or a couple of soft- or hard-boiled eggs.

SERVES 4

THAI *Red* *Vegetable* CURRY

1 tablespoon coconut oil or good-
    quality animal fat*
1 onion, chopped
2 tablespoons Thai red curry paste
    (for a recipe, see page 243)
600 ml coconut cream
300 ml vegetable stock or Chicken
    Bone Broth (page 234)
2 cm piece of ginger, finely sliced
½ lemongrass stalk, white part
    only, finely sliced
3 kaffir lime leaves, crushed
½ small red chilli, deseeded and
    chopped, plus extra to serve
    (optional)
1 large carrot, sliced
200 g broccoli, cut into florets
200 g cauliflower, cut into florets
2 Japanese eggplants, cut into 2 cm
    thick slices
6 shiitake or Swiss brown
    mushrooms, sliced
4 asparagus spears, trimmed and
    cut into 3 cm lengths
juice of ½ lime
fish sauce, to taste (optional)
sea salt and freshly ground black
    pepper
coriander and Thai basil leaves,
    to serve
Cauliflower Rice (page 233), to serve
lime wedges, to serve

* See Glossary

❶ Melt the oil or fat in a large saucepan over medium heat. Add the onion and cook for 5 minutes until softened. Add the curry paste and cook for 30 seconds until fragrant. Gradually stir in the coconut cream and stock or broth, then add the ginger, lemongrass, kaffir lime leaves and chilli (if using) and bring to a gentle simmer.

❷ Add the carrot, broccoli, cauliflower and eggplant to the pan and simmer for 20 minutes until the vegetables are tender and the sauce is reduced to a creamy consistency.

❸ Stir in the mushrooms and asparagus and cook for 5 minutes until the asparagus is tender. Remove from the heat.

❹ Mix in the lime juice and season to taste with a little fish sauce (if using) and salt and pepper.

❺ Ladle the curry straight into serving bowls and sprinkle on the coriander and Thai basil leaves and the extra chilli (if using). Serve with the cauliflower rice and lime wedges on the side.

PRESSURE COOKER Follow step ❶, using your pressure cooker over medium–high heat, but use only 210 ml of stock or broth rather than 300 ml. Add the carrot, broccoli, cauliflower and eggplant, close and lock the lid, then bring the cooker to high pressure over high heat. Reduce the heat to medium to maintain pressure and cook for 5 minutes. Let the pressure drop naturally before opening the lid. Follow steps ❸–❺.

SLOW COOKER Follow step ❶, but use only 210 ml of stock or broth rather than 300 ml. Transfer everything from the pan to your slow cooker. Add the carrot, broccoli, cauliflower and eggplant, cover and cook on low for 6 hours, or until the vegetables are tender. Add the mushrooms and asparagus, cover and cook on high for 30 minutes until tender. Follow steps ❹–❺.

As a young apprentice chef I worked in a few Italian restaurants and discovered the beauty of Italian food. This is a bit of a nod to those days. In this paleo version of risotto, I have replaced the rice with cauliflower, infused the whole dish with the flavour of mushrooms and finished it with chestnuts (you could use toasted pine nuts or walnuts instead). Stir through some cashew cheese at the end, if you like.

Wild Mushroom 'RISOTTO'
SERVES 4 WITH CHESTNUTS AND TRUFFLE OIL

1 tablespoon dried porcini mushrooms
600 g cauliflower, roughly chopped
3 tablespoons coconut oil or good-quality animal fat*
150 g king brown or oyster mushrooms, sliced
150 g Swiss brown mushrooms, sliced
200 g pine, slippery jack or portobello mushrooms, sliced
sea salt and freshly ground black pepper
1 onion, diced
4 garlic cloves, chopped
1 teaspoon finely chopped thyme
125 ml (½ cup) dry white wine
300 ml Beef or Chicken Bone Broth (pages 230 and 234) or vegetable stock
2 teaspoons lemon juice
2 tablespoons finely chopped flat-leaf parsley leaves, plus extra to serve
4 peeled chestnuts, finely sliced and toasted (see note)
truffle-infused olive oil or extra-virgin olive oil, to serve

* See Glossary

❶ Soak the porcini mushrooms in 100 ml of water for 10 minutes. Drain, reserving the mushroom water.

❷ To make the cauliflower rice, place the cauliflower in the bowl of a food processor and pulse into tiny, fine pieces that look like rice.

❸ Melt 1 tablespoon of the oil or fat in a saucepan over medium–high heat. Add the sliced mushrooms and sauté for 2 minutes, season with salt and pepper and remove from the pan. Wipe the pan clean, add the remaining coconut oil or fat and the onion and sauté for 5 minutes until the onion is translucent. Stir in the garlic, thyme and reserved porcini mushrooms and sauté for 30 seconds. Pour in the wine and cook until completely reduced, 5–10 minutes.

❹ Add the cauliflower rice, broth or stock and reserved mushroom water to the pan, return the mushrooms and cook, stirring occasionally, for 5–7 minutes until the cauliflower rice is cooked through. Remove from the heat, stir in the lemon juice and parsley and season with salt and pepper.

❺ To finish, divide the risotto between four serving plates, scatter over the chestnuts and extra parsley and drizzle with the truffle or extra-virgin olive oil.

Note
To prepare the chestnuts, score the top and bottom of each one with a knife and place on a baking tray. Roast in a 180°C oven for 10–12 minutes until the skins split. Transfer the hot roasted chestnuts to a small bowl, cover with plastic wrap and set aside for 10 minutes to steam. Peel away the hard outer layer and discard. Finely slice the chestnuts, transfer to a greased baking tray, drizzle over a little olive oil and toast in the oven at 180°C for 5–6 minutes until golden. Season with a little salt.

Lately cauliflower has become a bit of a rock star in the culinary scene. This is a simple curry recipe that I encourage you to double, as you will be heading to the fridge to eat any leftovers cold the next day. It's also delicious with some halved soft- or hard-boiled eggs stirred through.

Creamy CAULIFLOWER and Coconut CURRY

SERVES 4–6

2 tablespoons coconut oil or good-quality animal fat*

1 large head of cauliflower (about 800 g), cut into bite-sized florets

1 onion, chopped

1 teaspoon finely grated ginger

2 garlic cloves, chopped

1 teaspoon black mustard seeds (yellow or brown mustard seeds are also good)

1½ tablespoons garam masala

1½ teaspoons ground turmeric

1–2 pinches of cayenne pepper (optional)

15 fresh curry leaves

600 ml coconut cream

200 ml Chicken Bone Broth (page 234) or water

sea salt and freshly ground black pepper

juice of 1 lemon

See Glossary

❶ Heat 1 tablespoon of the oil or fat in a large frying pan over medium–high heat. Add the cauliflower in batches and cook for 5 minutes until lightly golden. Remove the cauliflower from the pan.

❷ Add the remaining oil or fat and the onion to the pan and cook, stirring occasionally, for 5 minutes, or until the onion is translucent. Add the ginger, garlic and mustard seeds and cook, stirring constantly, for 20–30 seconds until the mustard seeds start to pop. Reduce the heat to medium–low, stir in the ground spices and cook for 15 seconds until fragrant.

❸ Add the curry leaves to the pan and cook for 10 seconds. Pour in the coconut cream and broth or water, return the cauliflower to the pan and stir to combine.

❹ Reduce the heat to low, cover with a lid and cook for 30 minutes until the cauliflower is tender and the sauce has thickened slightly.

❺ Season with salt and pepper. Stir through the lemon juice and serve.

PRESSURE COOKER Follow steps ❶–❷, using your pressure cooker over medium–high heat. Follow step ❸, but use only 100 ml of broth or water rather than 200 ml. Close and lock the lid, then bring the cooker to high pressure over high heat. Reduce the heat to medium to maintain pressure and cook for 5 minutes. Release the pressure using the quick release method (see page 11) before opening the lid. Follow step ❺.

SLOW COOKER Follow steps ❶–❷. Add the curry leaves and cook for another 10 seconds, then transfer everything in the pan to your slow cooker. Pour in the coconut cream and only 100 ml of broth or water. Cover and cook on low for 6 hours, or until the cauliflower is tender. Follow step ❺.

If you are a fan of Indian food, you might enjoy the vibrant spinach curry, palak paneer. Here is my paleo version. I have replaced the paneer cheese with swede (I've gotta say, swede has a lot more nutritional value than cheese) and cooked it in the same way, coating the swede in delicious green sauce. Feel free to swap out the swede for turnip, sweet potato or pumpkin.

SWEDE and Spinach CURRY

SERVES 2

300 g baby spinach leaves

2 tablespoons coriander leaves

500 ml (2 cups) Chicken Bone Broth (page 234) or water

sea salt

4 swedes, cut into 2 cm cubes

2 tablespoons coconut oil or good-quality animal fat*

3 large garlic cloves, finely chopped

2 teaspoons finely grated ginger

½ teaspoon cumin seeds

1 teaspoon ground cumin

1 teaspoon ground coriander

½ teaspoon garam masala

1–2 pinches of cayenne pepper

2 tablespoons coconut cream

juice of ½ lemon

freshly ground black pepper

Raita

½ Lebanese cucumber

200 g coconut yoghurt (for a recipe, see page 235)

1 teaspoon ground cumin

2 tablespoons finely chopped mint leaves

sea salt and freshly ground black pepper

* See Glossary

❶ To make the raita, cut the cucumber in half lengthways and use a teaspoon to scrape out the seeds. Coarsely grate the cucumber flesh and squeeze out the excess liquid with your hands. Combine the cucumber with the yoghurt, cumin and mint in a bowl and stir well. Season to taste.

❷ Place the spinach, coriander leaves, 250 ml of the broth or water and a pinch of salt in the bowl of a food processor and puree.

❸ Place the swede in a saucepan of boiling water. Turn the heat down to low and simmer for 15 minutes, or until the swede is tender. Drain, then transfer to a large bowl. Keep warm.

❹ Heat the oil or fat in the same pan. Add the garlic, ginger and cumin seeds and cook for 30 seconds until fragrant. Stir in the ground cumin, ground coriander, garam masala and cayenne pepper and cook for another minute.

❺ Add the pureed spinach and some salt to the pan, then pour in the remaining broth or water and the coconut cream and cook for 2 minutes. Stir in the boiled swede and cook for a further minute until heated through. Squeeze over the lemon juice and season with salt and pepper. Serve with the raita on the side and a side of cauliflower, if desired.

PRESSURE COOKER Follow steps ❶–❷. Place the swede in your pressure cooker and cover with water. Close and lock the lid, bring the cooker to high pressure and cook for 10 minutes over medium–high heat. Release the pressure before opening the lid, then drain the swede and transfer to a large bowl. Follow steps ❹–❺, with your pressure cooker on medium–high heat.

Chapter Two
SEAFOOD

Sometimes the simplest dishes are the best, and, for some lip-slurping goodness, you can't get much simpler than this Italian-flavoured baked fish and clams. I have used broccolini here but you could quite easily use fresh tomatoes, fennel, roasted capsicum, silverbeet, spinach or kale. Serve with a delicious salad and some fermented veg. Oh, and some kalamata olives would also be awesome.

Herbed BARRAMUNDI *and* CLAM BAKE

SERVES 2–4

2 × 200 g barramundi fillets (or other white-fleshed fish, such as snapper or flathead), skin removed

sea salt and freshly ground black pepper

4 tablespoons coconut oil or good-quality animal fat*

1 bunch of broccolini (about 180 g), chopped

4 garlic cloves, finely chopped

1–2 long red chillies, deseeded and finely chopped

3 salted anchovy fillets, rinsed, patted dry and very finely chopped

grated zest and juice of 1 lemon

3 tablespoons finely chopped flat-leaf parsley leaves

3 tablespoons dry white wine

125 ml (½ cup) Fish or Chicken Bone Broth (pages 237 and 234) or water

25 vongole (clams), cleaned

See Glossary

❶ Preheat the oven to 180°C.

❷ Lightly season the fish fillets with salt and pepper. Melt 2 tablespoons of the oil or fat in a flameproof casserole dish over high heat. Add the fish and cook briefly on each side until lightly golden, about 30 seconds. Remove from the dish and set aside.

❸ Reduce the heat to medium, add the remaining oil or fat and the broccolini to the dish and cook for 1 minute, then add the garlic and fry for 30 seconds until lightly coloured. Stir in the chilli, anchovies, lemon zest and parsley and fry for 30 seconds until fragrant. Pour in the wine and broth or water and remove from the heat.

❹ Return the fish to the dish in a single layer, then scatter the vongole around the fish. Cover the dish and bake for 12 minutes, or until the vongole have opened and the fish is cooked through. Season with salt and pepper.

❺ Drizzle over the lemon juice and serve.

I love reinventing classic recipes. Here, I take the famous Southern USA dish perloo and replace the rice with cauliflower. Perloo is a bit like a jambalaya or paella; wonderful spices and vegetables are cooked and then some broth and protein are added, before being served family style at the dinner table. I have included oysters, but you could use mussels, clams, squid, fish, scallops or crab, separately or all together.

SERVES 4 PRAWN *Perloo*

3 tablespoons coconut oil or good-quality animal fat*

4 paleo pork sausages

2 onions, chopped

200 g ham, finely chopped

1½ red capsicums, chopped

1 jalapeno chilli, deseeded and chopped

¼ teaspoon chilli powder or a few pinches of cayenne pepper (optional)

1 teaspoon smoked paprika

sea salt and freshly ground black pepper

3 tomatoes, roughly chopped

3 garlic cloves, finely chopped

2 tablespoons chopped flat-leaf parsley leaves

3 thyme sprigs, leaves picked and finely chopped

500 g uncooked Cauliflower Rice (page 233)

2 silverbeet leaves, stalks removed, leaves chopped

250 ml (1 cup) Chicken Bone Broth (page 234)

12 raw large prawns, shelled and deveined with heads and tails intact

20 freshly shucked rock or pacific oysters, removed from shells

lemon wedges, to serve (optional)

* See Glossary

❶ Melt 1 tablespoon of the oil or fat in a large frying pan over medium heat. Add the sausages and cook, tossing occasionally, for 8–10 minutes until almost cooked through. Remove the sausages from the pan, place on a chopping board and, when cool enough to handle, cut into bite-sized pieces.

❷ Add the remaining oil or fat and the onion to the pan and sauté for 6–8 minutes until the onion is translucent. Add the ham, capsicum, chilli, chilli powder or cayenne pepper (if using) and smoked paprika and cook, stirring occasionally, for 6 minutes until the capsicum is softened. Season with salt and pepper

❸ Reduce the heat to medium, add the tomato, garlic, parsley and thyme and cook for 4 minutes until the tomato has broken down slightly. Add the sausages, cauliflower rice and silverbeet, pour in the broth and stir. Place the prawns on top in a single layer, cover and cook for 3–4 minutes until the prawns change colour. Flip the prawns over then scatter over the oysters and cook, covered, for 1 minute until the oysters are heated through and the prawns are just cooked. Season with salt and pepper if needed.

❹ Serve with the lemon wedges on the side if you like.

Tip Make sure you save the stalks from your silverbeet and parsley. They're perfect for adding to broths, stocks and soups.

There is something magical about this dish and the depth of flavour that develops. You marinate the fish, cook it at the start, remove it so that it's not overcooked and then add it back in at the end to finish cooking in the amazing curry sauce. These simple little techniques ensure you have a moist yet flavoursome dish. I have teamed this with zucchini rice, but feel free to try cauliflower or broccoli rice instead.

SERVES 4 *Bengali* FISH

600 g mulloway, blue-eye trevalla, snapper or other white-fleshed fish fillets, skin removed, flesh cut into 3 cm pieces
4 tablespoons coconut oil or good-quality animal fat*
500 g cauliflower, broken into florets
1 large onion, finely chopped
2 small green chillies, deseeded and finely chopped, plus extra to serve
2 garlic cloves, finely chopped
2 teaspoons finely grated ginger
1 teaspoon mustard seeds
2 teaspoons ground coriander
1 teaspoon ground turmeric
1–2 pinches of cayenne pepper (optional)
3 tablespoons tomato paste
500 ml (2 cups) Fish or Chicken Bone Broth (pages 237 and 234)
sea salt and freshly ground black pepper
a few coriander sprigs, to serve
Zucchini Rice (page 245), to serve

Marinade
1½ teaspoons ground coriander
1 teaspoon ground turmeric
½ teaspoon mustard powder
½ teaspoon sea salt
1 tablespoon lemon juice
pinch of cayenne pepper

See Glossary

❶ For the marinade, place all the ingredients in a bowl and mix to combine. Add the fish and coat in the marinade. Cover with plastic wrap and transfer to the fridge for 15 minutes.

❷ Heat 2 tablespoons of oil or fat in a large frying pan over medium–high heat until just starting to smoke. Add the fish and cook for 1 minute on each side, or until golden but still raw in the centre. Remove from the pan and set aside.

❸ Reduce the heat to medium, add 1 tablespoon of the oil or fat and the cauliflower and sauté for 5–6 minutes, or until the cauliflower is lightly golden. Remove from the pan and set aside.

❹ Melt the remaining oil or fat in the pan, add the onion and cook, stirring occasionally, for 5–6 minutes until translucent. Add the chilli and garlic and cook for 30 seconds until softened, then add the ginger, mustard seeds, ground coriander, turmeric and cayenne pepper (if using) and cook, stirring, for 30 seconds until fragrant. Stir in the tomato paste and cook for a further 30 seconds.

❺ Pour the broth into the pan, mix to combine and bring to the boil. Reduce the heat to low, return the cauliflower to the pan, cover and simmer for 15 minutes until the cauliflower is tender. Return the fish to the pan and cook for 2–3 minutes until the fish is cooked through. Season with salt and pepper. Scatter on the coriander sprigs and serve with the zucchini rice on the side.

This delicious herb-coated fish and broth dish is full of wonderful aromatic flavours that will have your tastebuds celebrating every spoonful. If you like, you can add prawns or seafood to the broth to make it a seafood celebration, and feel free to include other vegetables, depending on what is in season or what you have on hand.

HERB-CRUSTED FISH

SERVES 4 *with Native Greens*

600 g snapper fillet, skin removed
sea salt and freshly ground
   black pepper
100 g oyster mushrooms, torn
50 g shimeji mushrooms
fish sauce, to taste
juice of 1 lime
100 g samphire* or other native
   greens (or spinach or asparagus)
1 small red chilli, deseeded and
   finely sliced

Broth
1 teaspoon coconut oil
2 French shallots, finely chopped
1 celery stalk, finely chopped
1 lemongrass stalk, white part only,
   bruised and roughly chopped
5 cm piece of ginger, finely sliced
125 ml (½ cup) dry white wine
750 ml (3 cups) Fish or Chicken
   Bone Broth (pages 237 and 234)
2 kaffir lime leaves, torn
1 long red chilli, halved lengthways

Herb crust
3 garlic cloves, finely grated
1 long red chilli, deseeded and
   finely chopped
2 very large handfuls of finely
   chopped coriander and mint leaves
2 tablespoons coconut oil, melted

See Glossary

❶ To make the broth, heat the oil in a large, deep frying pan over medium heat. Add the shallot and celery and cook, stirring occasionally, for 5 minutes until the vegetables are soft. Add the lemongrass and ginger and cook for 1 minute until fragrant. Pour in the wine and broth, add the lime leaves and chilli and bring to the boil. Turn the heat down to low and simmer for 20 minutes. Remove from the heat and cool the broth until lukewarm, then strain through a sieve into a jug and set aside until needed.

❷ Meanwhile, cut the fish into four equal pieces and season with salt and pepper.

❸ To make the herb crust, combine all the ingredients in a small bowl with a little salt and mix.

❹ Spread the herb crust evenly on top of each piece of fish. Place the fish in the pan, add the mushrooms, then pour in enough broth to reach two-thirds of the way up the side of the fish. (It's important not to fully submerge the fish or the crust will fall off.) Cover with a lid and cook over low heat for 8–10 minutes until the fish is cooked through.

❺ Carefully remove the fish from the pan and place in shallow serving bowls.

❻ Pour the remaining stock into the pan, bring to a simmer, then remove from the heat. Add fish sauce to taste and stir in the lime juice. Divide the mushrooms and samphire between the bowls, pour in the broth and serve with the chilli.

Tip Any firm, white-fleshed fish fillets will work well in this recipe – try blue-eye trevalla or ling.

I love cooking and serving whole fish – the theatre of it is awesome and the flesh retains a lot more moisture and flavour. For a family with young kids, serving fish on the bone can be troublesome, so feel free to use fillets instead, and simply reduce the cooking time. I use barramundi here, but snapper, bream, flathead, whiting, salmon or trout or, if you are super lucky, coral trout are equally as good.

Whole BARRAMUNDI *with*
SERVES 2–3   CORIANDER, GINGER AND GALANGAL

2 whole barramundi (about 600 g each), cleaned, scaled and gutted
sea salt
3 tablespoons coconut oil
2 red Asian shallots, finely diced
1 long red chilli, deseeded and finely chopped
10 coriander stalks, finely chopped
1 large handful of coriander leaves, plus extra to serve
½ bunch of kale (about 200 g), stalks removed, leaves chopped
2 spring onions, finely sliced, plus extra to serve
250 ml (1 cup) Fish Bone Broth (page 237) or water
freshly ground black pepper

Spice rub
5 garlic cloves, chopped
3 red Asian shallots, finely chopped
3 tablespoons finely grated ginger
1½ tablespoons finely grated galangal*
grated zest of 1 lime
segments of 1 lime
1 teaspoon finely grated fresh turmeric (or ¼ teaspoon ground turmeric)
3 teaspoons fish sauce

* See Glossary

❶ To make the spice rub, combine the garlic, shallot, ginger, galangal, lime zest and segments and turmeric and use a mortar and pestle or food processor to form a coarse paste. Mix in the fish sauce.

❷ Place the barramundi on a plate, season with a touch of salt, then rub the spice paste all over, inside and out, to evenly coat. Cover with plastic wrap and marinate in the fridge for 20 minutes.

❸ Melt the oil in a large wok or frying pan over medium–high heat. Add the shallot and chilli and sauté for 1 minute until fragrant. Add the barramundi, coriander stalks and leaves, kale and spring onion and cook for 2 minutes. Flip the fish over and cook for a further 2 minutes. Pour in the broth or water and bring to the boil. Cover the pan, reduce the heat to medium–low and simmer for 10 minutes until the fish is cooked through. Season with salt and pepper, if needed. Serve straight from the pan or transfer to a platter and scatter the extra coriander leaves and spring onions over the top. Add an extra splash of fish sauce if needed.

I tried this dish many years ago at Michael White's NYC restaurant Marca on Central Park. And Michael, an amazing chef with the best Italian restaurants in the USA, has kindly shared his recipe. Instead of serving the octopus and bone marrow with pasta, I think they are awesome on their own or tossed with some delicious zucchini or parsnip noodles. Thanks Michael, you are a champ.

Braised OCTOPUS
SERVES 4–6 WITH BONE MARROW

2 tablespoons coconut oil or
   good-quality animal fat*
1 onion, diced
1 celery stalk, diced
4 garlic cloves, finely chopped
1 long red chilli, deseeded and finely
   chopped (optional)
1 bay leaf
2 thyme sprigs, leaves picked
1 kg tentacles from a medium–large
   octopus, chopped into 5 cm
   pieces
250 ml (1 cup) full-bodied,
   preservative-free red wine
2 × 400 g cans whole peeled
   tomatoes (or 800 g tomatoes,
   diced)
100 g kalamata olives, pitted and
   halved
30 g salted baby capers, rinsed and
   patted dry
125 ml (½ cup) Fish or Chicken Bone
   Broth (pages 237 and 234) or
   water
sea salt and freshly ground
   black pepper
200 g bone marrow, roughly chopped
baby basil leaves, to serve

* See Glossary

❶ Heat the oil or fat in a large, heavy-based saucepan over medium–high heat. Add the onion, celery, garlic, chilli (if using) and herbs, reduce the heat to medium and sauté for 3–5 minutes. Add the octopus and cook for 5 minutes, or until the tentacles are opaque and release some liquid. Pour in the wine and cook until reduced by half. Stir in the tomatoes, olives, capers and broth or water and season with salt and pepper.

❷ Reduce the heat to low and simmer, covered, for 1½ hours until the octopus is tender.

❸ Remove the lid and continue to simmer over low heat for 5–10 minutes until reduced to a coating consistency.

❹ Stir through the bone marrow and simmer for 5 minutes until cooked through. Garnish with some baby basil leaves and serve.

PRESSURE COOKER Place your pressure cooker over medium heat and follow step ❶, but add only 3 tablespoons of broth or water rather than 125 ml. Close and lock the lid, bring the cooker to high pressure, then reduce the heat to medium to maintain pressure and cook for 20 minutes. Let the pressure drop naturally before opening the lid. Follow steps ❸–❹, cooking over medium heat.

SLOW COOKER Follow step ❶, but add only 3 tablespoons of broth or water rather than 125 ml. Transfer the sautéed vegetables, herbs, octopus and liquid from the pan to your slow cooker. Cover and cook on low for 9 hours, or until the octopus is tender. Add the bone marrow to your slow cooker, cover and cook on low for 10–15 minutes. Garnish with some baby basil leaves before serving.

When summer hits it's prawn season for us at home. I am always looking for interesting ways to turn these delicious creatures of the sea into a taste sensation. Here, to elevate the dish to another level, we take a wonderfully aromatic Sri Lankan-inspired curry sauce and add the prawns. The key with prawns is not to overcook them, as they can become tough and rubbery and lose their flavour.

Sri Lankan
PRAWNS
SERVES 4

2 teaspoons cumin seeds

45 g (¾ cup) shredded coconut

1 teaspoon whole black peppercorns

½ teaspoon ground turmeric

2 tablespoons coconut oil

1 teaspoon yellow mustard seeds

1 teaspoon fennel seeds

1 onion, finely chopped

4 garlic cloves, finely chopped

14 fresh curry leaves (about 1 sprig)

1 long red chilli, deseeded and
    finely chopped

1 tablespoon mild curry powder

½ teaspoon chilli powder

600 ml coconut cream

1½ teaspoons tamarind puree*

4 kaffir lime leaves, torn

12 raw large prawns, shelled
    and deveined with heads and
    tails intact

juice of 1 lime

sea salt

2 tablespoons chopped coriander
    leaves

* See Glossary

❶ Combine the cumin seeds, coconut and peppercorns in a large, heavy-based saucepan over medium heat and toast, tossing occasionally, for 30–60 seconds until the coconut is golden brown and fragrant. Remove from the pan and allow to cool.

❷ Using a mortar and pestle or spice grinder, grind the cumin seed mixture to a coarse powder, then mix in the turmeric. Set aside.

❸ Melt the oil in the pan over medium heat. Add the mustard seeds and fennel seeds and cook until the mustard seeds start to pop. Stir in the onion, garlic, curry leaves and chilli and cook for a few minutes until the onion is soft.

❹ Add the curry powder, chilli powder and turmeric spice mixture and cook for 1 minute, stirring constantly to ensure the spices do not burn.

❺ Stir the coconut cream, tamarind puree, kaffir lime leaves and 120 ml of water into the pan and bring to the boil. Reduce the heat to low and simmer for 15 minutes.

❻ Add the prawns to the pan to simmer for a further 2 minutes until they are just cooked. Remove from the heat, add the lime juice and season with salt. Scatter over the coriander and serve.

I love to travel to Malaysia, mainly because I know I am going to eat like a king when I am there. Malaysian cuisine is among the best in the world in my eyes and the flavours generated through the use of spices are mind- and tastebud-blowing. Here we have fresh curry leaves, lime leaves, lemongrass, turmeric and, of course, garlic and chilli to excite the palate.

Malaysian FISH CURRY

SERVES 4–6

2 tablespoons coconut oil

2 onions, chopped

4 kaffir lime leaves, torn

16 fresh curry leaves

500 g kent pumpkin, cut into
2.5 cm cubes

1 cinnamon stick

1 lemongrass stalk, white part only,
bruised with the back of a knife
and cut into 5 cm pieces

3 star anise

1 × 400 ml can coconut cream

375 ml (1½ cups) Fish or Chicken
Bone Broth (pages 237 and 234)
or water

900 g snapper, rockling, mulloway
or other white-fleshed fish fillets,
skin removed, flesh pin-boned
and cut into 2.5 cm pieces

2 tablespoons fish sauce

sea salt and freshly ground
black pepper

1 tablespoon lime juice

Curry paste

5 garlic cloves

3 long red chillies, deseeded and
chopped

2 lemongrass stalks, white part
only, finely chopped

1½ tablespoons finely grated ginger

4 red Asian shallots, finely chopped

1 teaspoon ground turmeric

2 tablespoons fish sauce

① To make the curry paste, place all the ingredients in a blender, add 3 tablespoons of water and blend to a smooth paste. Add a little more water if needed.

② Heat the oil in a large saucepan over medium heat. Add the onion and cook, stirring occasionally, for 5 minutes until the onion is translucent. Stir in the curry paste and cook for 2 minutes until fragrant. Add the kaffir lime leaves, curry leaves, pumpkin, cinnamon, lemongrass, star anise, coconut cream and broth or water. Bring to a simmer, reduce the heat to low and cook for 30 minutes until the flavours have developed and the pumpkin is cooked.

③ Add the fish to the curry sauce and cook for 5–8 minutes until the fish is cooked through.

④ Season with the fish sauce and a little salt and pepper, gently stir in the lime juice and serve.

This delicious dish is based on an old chilli crab recipe. I have made it paleo by suggesting you make your own paleo versions of tomato ketchup, hoisin sauce and sweet chilli sauce. Sure you can use pre-made versions if you choose to, but read the ingredients list so you are aware of what you are popping into your system. If you can't find good crabs, this dish works really well with prawns, lobsters and mussels.

SERVES 2

Chilli MUD CRAB

2 × 1.5 kg live mud crabs

2½ tablespoons coconut oil

4 garlic cloves, chopped

2 long red chillies, deseeded and chopped

2 tablespoons julienned ginger

1 tablespoon chopped coriander stalks and roots

120 ml Tomato Ketchup (page 243)

4 tablespoons Paleo Sweet Chilli Sauce (page 240)

190 ml Chicken Bone Broth (page 234)

3 tablespoons Paleo Hoisin Sauce (page 240)

1 tablespoon fish sauce

1–2 tablespoons coconut sugar (optional)

250 g cherry tomatoes, cut in half

1 teaspoon sea salt

1 spring onion, green part only, finely sliced

1 handful of mixed mint, Vietnamese mint and coriander leaves

❶ To prepare the mud crabs, place them in the freezer for 1–2 hours. Remove the top shell by lifting the flap on the underside. Clean away the spongy grey gills and any other non-fleshy parts and rinse very lightly and quickly under cold running water.

❷ Using a cleaver, cut the crabs in half lengthways, then cut each half into three. Crack the claws with the back of the cleaver to expose the crabmeat (this helps the flesh absorb the sauce when cooking).

❸ Heat the oil in a large wok or saucepan over medium–high heat and cook the garlic, chilli, ginger and coriander stalks and roots until fragrant. Add the crab pieces and toss for 1–2 minutes until they change colour. Add the tomato ketchup, chilli sauce, broth, hoisin sauce, fish sauce and coconut sugar (if using), stir well and bring to the boil. Cover and simmer for 5 minutes, then add the cherry tomatoes and simmer for a further 5 minutes until slightly softened. Stir through the salt.

❹ Add the spring onion and herbs to the wok or pan. Remove from the heat and serve immediately at a table set with crab crackers, crab pickers, fingerbowls of warm water and lemon, and bibs.

Tip If you want to make this dish even more luscious, add a couple of whisked eggs at the end of step ❸ to lightly coat the crab.

Seamus Mullen, a very dear friend, is one of the USA's most famous chefs. Seamus suffered from rheumatoid arthritis until a few years ago. With the help of a doctor and a paleo-inspired approach to food, he was able to get off his drugs and get out of bed, and he now mountain bikes all around the world! When Seamus cooked this curry for me, the addition of avocado had me puzzled until I tried it. I gotta say, it was a revelation.

SEAFOOD CURRY

SERVES 4–6 *with Avocado*

3 tablespoons coconut oil

450 g white-fleshed fish fillets, skin removed, cut into 2.5 cm pieces

8 scallops

sea salt and freshly ground black pepper

2 red Asian shallots, finely sliced

4 garlic cloves, finely chopped

2.5 cm piece of ginger, julienned

1 serrano chilli, deseeded and chopped

300 g Japanese pumpkin, peeled and cut into 2 cm pieces

2 carrots, cut into 1 cm slices

100 g oyster mushrooms

2 lemongrass stalks, white part only, bruised with the back of a knife

1 tablespoon apple cider vinegar

2 × 400 ml cans coconut milk

1 teaspoon fish sauce

2 baby bok choy, halved

1 handful of samphire* (optional)

750 g mussels, scrubbed and debearded

juice of 1 lime

2 spring onions, finely sliced

1 handful of coriander leaves, torn

1 handful of mint leaves, torn

1 avocado, diced

2 teaspoons black chia seeds

* See Glossary

❶ Heat 1 tablespoon of the oil in a large saucepan over high heat. Season the fish and scallops with salt and pepper and sear on each side for 1 minute. Remove from the pan and set aside.

❷ Reduce the heat to medium, add the remaining oil, then add the shallot, garlic, ginger and chilli and cook for 2 minutes. Add the pumpkin and carrot to the pan and cook for 2 minutes until starting to colour. Add the mushrooms and lemongrass and sauté for a further 2 minutes until the mushrooms soften. Deglaze with the vinegar, pour in the coconut milk and fish sauce, season with salt and pepper and simmer for 10 minutes until the vegetables are soft.

❸ Add the seared fish and gently poach for 2 minutes.

❹ Add the bok choy, samphire (if using), mussels and seared scallops to the pan. Cover and cook until the mussels have opened.

❺ Add a squeeze of lime juice, scatter over the spring onion, coriander, mint and avocado and sprinkle with the chia seeds to serve.

I usually like to buy a kilogram of mussels every week, as they are one of the most nutrient-dense foods and I am always looking for new ways to cook them. If you are new to eating mussels, I urge you to give this moreish recipe a try. To bulk the dish out, you can add in prawns or other seafood and serve over a small bowl of coconut cauliflower rice for that wonderful textural element.

MUSSELS WITH RED CURRY SAUCE
and Eggplant

SERVES 2

1 tablespoon coconut oil or
   good-quality animal fat*
2 garlic cloves, finely chopped
1 tablespoon finely grated ginger
1½ tablespoons Thai red curry paste
   (for a recipe, see page 243)
400 ml coconut cream
2 kaffir lime leaves, torn
1 teaspoon coconut sugar
200 g Thai eggplants, stems
   removed (or regular eggplant,
   diced)
1 kg mussels, scrubbed and
   debearded
coriander and Thai basil leaves,
   to serve
lime wedges, to serve

* See Glossary

❶ Heat the oil or fat in a large saucepan over medium heat. Add the garlic, ginger and curry paste and cook, stirring frequently, for 2 minutes until fragrant.

❷ Pour in the coconut cream, then add the lime leaves and coconut sugar and stir to combine. Bring to the boil, reduce the heat to low and simmer for 8 minutes.

❸ Add the Thai eggplants to the pan and cook for 6 minutes, or until they are almost cooked through. Add the mussels, stir, then increase the heat to medium–high, cover with a lid and cook for 3–4 minutes until the mussels open. Spoon into warm bowls, top with the coriander and Thai basil leaves and serve with the lime wedges on the side.

Tip If you don't have time to make your own curry paste, it's fine to use a store-bought version – just check to make sure it doesn't contain any sugar, soybeans or gluten.

My dear friends Cortney Burns and her partner Nick Balla run the kitchen at Bar Tartine in San Francisco. Cortney and I have worked together a few times on different TV programs in the States, including my cooking series *The Paleo Way*, where she cooked this dish that blew me away. Based on a Hungarian fish stew, it packs a ton of flavour and will have you asking for a second serve ... and maybe a third.

Green FISHERMAN'S Stew

SERVES 4

3 large handfuls of flat-leaf parsley leaves, plus extra to serve

2 litres (8 cups) Fish Bone Broth (page 237)

2 teaspoons coconut oil or good-quality animal fat*

2 small pickling onions, finely sliced

8 garlic cloves, finely sliced

80 g wood ear fungus*, stalks removed

80 g oyster mushrooms, stalks removed

1 fennel bulb (about 225 g), halved, cored and finely sliced

1½ teaspoons sea salt

1 tablespoon green chilli powder (or 1½ teaspoons red chilli powder)

450 g catfish, basa fish or other white-fleshed fish fillets, skin removed, cut into 1 cm thick pieces

120 g young collard greens or silverbeet, stalks removed, torn into 2.5 cm pieces

3 tablespoons fish sauce

12 salted anchovy fillets, rinsed and patted dry, finely chopped

1 lemon, halved

2 spring onions, white and tender green parts, finely sliced

freshly ground black pepper

* See Glossary

❶ Combine the parsley and 500 ml of the broth in a blender or food processor and puree until smooth. Set aside.

❷ Heat a deep frying pan or saucepan over medium heat until a drop of water flicked on the surface sizzles gently on contact. Add the oil or fat, onion, garlic, wood ear, mushroom, fennel and 1 teaspoon of the salt and cook, stirring occasionally, until the vegetables are soft, about 10 minutes. Add the chilli powder and stir until fragrant, about 1 minute.

❸ Pour in the remaining broth, then add the fish, collard greens or silverbeet, fish sauce, anchovies and remaining salt. Simmer until the fish is cooked, about 5 minutes. (The fish will fall apart if cooked for more than 5 minutes or stirred too vigorously.) Stir in the pureed parsley and remove from the heat.

❹ Ladle the stew into serving bowls. Tear the extra parsley leaves and scatter over each portion. Squeeze on some lemon juice, sprinkle on the spring onion and pepper and add a little more salt if needed.

This beautifully poached rainbow trout in broth is another dish from my dear friend Cortney Burns, and it has to be tasted to understand how good it actually is. Here, we crisp up the skin on the trout and, for a short amount of time, gently simmer it in a delicious dashi broth with some shiitake mushrooms and pickled mustard greens, before finishing with some chilli oil and coconut oil.

RAINBOW TROUT *with*

SERVES 4 · PICKLED GREENS AND MUSHROOMS

4 × 100 g rainbow trout fillets, skin left on, pin-boned

1 teaspoon coconut oil, melted

sea salt

1 litre (4 cups) Strong Dashi (page 242)

350 g (1 cup) chopped Pickled Chinese Mustard Greens (page 241) (fresh choy sum, bok choy or kale will also work well if you don't have these pickles to hand)

100 g baby or large quartered shiitake mushrooms, stems removed

2 tablespoons Chilli Oil (page 235), warmed

2 tablespoons coconut oil, warmed

4 spring onions, finely sliced on the diagonal

1 handful of flat-leaf parsley leaves, torn

❶ Heat a large, heavy-based non-stick frying pan over high heat for 2 minutes until very hot. (This will prevent the skin of the fish from sticking to the pan.) Pat the skin of the trout with paper towel to remove any moisture, brush with the melted oil and season with a little salt. Cook, skin-side down and pressing down on the fish with a spatula, for 1 minute until the skin is crispy and charred. Remove from the pan and place on a plate.

❷ Wipe the pan clean, then pour in the dashi. Add the pickled mustard greens and mushrooms and bring to a simmer. Remove the green and mushrooms and divide between serving bowls.

❸ Add the fish to the dashi and gently poach over low heat with skin facing up for 30–60 seconds until just cooked through. Carefully remove the fillets with a spatula, place in the serving bowls and spoon over the dashi.

❹ Drizzle over the chilli oil and coconut oil. Top with the spring onion and parsley and serve immediately.

The intoxicating aroma of lemongrass cooking is enough to make you want to grow your own so you can eat it a few times a week. Here is a dish that really makes lemongrass shine. This simple Thai yellow curry is so comforting and warming it will become a firm family favourite. Feel free to add more seafood if you'd like – mussels, clams, squid, prawns, scallops or crab all work well.

Thai FISH CURRY

2 tablespoons coconut oil or
  good-quality animal fat*

1 onion, chopped

2 garlic cloves, chopped

1 tablespoon finely grated ginger

1 lemongrass stalk, white part only,
  finely chopped

1–2 long red chillies, deseeded and
  finely sliced

2 tablespoons yellow curry paste
  (for a recipe, see page 245)

1 red capsicum, chopped

28 fresh curry leaves (about 2 sprigs)

600 ml coconut cream

150 ml Fish Bone Broth (page 237)
  or water

800 g barramundi fillets, skin left
  on, cut into 4 cm pieces

sea salt and freshly ground
  black pepper

fish sauce (optional)

juice of 1 lime

Cauliflower Rice (page 233), to serve

lime wedges, to serve

See Glossary

❶ Melt the oil or fat in a large, deep frying pan over medium heat. Add the onion and cook, stirring occasionally, for 5–8 minutes until translucent. Add the garlic, ginger, lemongrass and chilli and cook for 30 seconds until softened and fragrant. Stir in the curry paste and cook for a further minute until the oil separates and comes to the surface. Add the capsicum and cook for few minutes to soften. Stir in the curry leaves, coconut cream and broth or water and bring to the boil, then reduce the heat to low and simmer gently for 5 minutes.

❷ Season the fish with salt and pepper, then gently stir into the curry sauce. Cover with a lid and cook for 7 minutes, or until the fish is cooked through.

❸ Season the curry with some more salt or fish sauce and pepper if needed, then stir in the lime juice. Serve with the cauliflower rice and lime wedges on the side.

Whenever I travel in Italy I am always drawn to the dramatic coastal seaside towns and villages that create simple yet exquisite seafood dishes. Here, I pay homage to those age-old traditions that respect seafood and the art of cooking. This unadulterated stew will be a welcome addition to any dinner table. Serve with some delicious vegetables or a salad on the side. And don't forget your fermented veg.

SERVES 4

Hearty Seafood STEW

2 tablespoons coconut oil or
   good-quality animal fat*
2 French shallots, chopped
4 garlic cloves, sliced
4 tomatoes, deseeded and roughly
   chopped
2 pinches of saffron threads
1 teaspoon thyme leaves
1 tablespoon pastis (such as
   Pernod) (optional)
175 ml (scant ¾ cup) dry white wine
2 baby squid, including tentacles,
   cleaned, scored and cut into
   2.5 cm pieces
4 raw king prawns, peeled and
   deveined with tails intact
400 g snapper fillets, skin on, cut
   into 2.5 cm pieces
250 ml (1 cup) Fish or Chicken Bone
   Broth (pages 237 and 234) or
   water, plus extra if needed
sea salt and freshly ground
   black pepper
8 mussels, scrubbed and debearded
12 vongole (clams), soaked in salted
   water for 1 hour, rinsed well
flat-leaf parsley leaves and dill
   fronds, torn, to serve

* See Glossary

❶ Melt the oil or fat in a large, heavy-based saucepan over medium heat. Add the shallot and garlic and cook gently for 5 minutes until soft. Stir in the tomato, saffron and thyme, add the pastis (if using) and wine and simmer until reduced by one-third, about 4–6 minutes.

❷ Add the squid, prawns and snapper to the pan and pour in enough broth or water to just cover the seafood. Season with salt and pepper and simmer for 2–4 minutes.

❸ Add the mussels and vongole to the pan, cover with a lid and cook for 2–4 minutes until the mussels and vongole open. Finish with a sprinkle of parsley and dill and serve.

There are a few constants that make up a great dish: the balance between fat, salt, spice, acid and sweetness; the texture; the aroma and, finally, the presentation. I tend to focus on the flavour, texture and aroma and, when it comes to presentation, take care to make the dish look attractive. Here is a delicious prawn and tomato curry that ticks all the above boxes.

PRAWN *and* Tomato CURRY

SERVES 4

3 tablespoons coconut oil or good-quality animal fat*
800 g raw king prawns, shelled and deveined with heads and tails intact
4 red Asian shallots, finely chopped
3 garlic cloves, finely chopped
1–2 long red chillies, deseeded and sliced (optional)
½ teaspoon ground turmeric
1 teaspoon ground coriander
1 × 400 g can diced tomatoes (or 400 g tomatoes, diced)
250 ml (1 cup) Fish Bone Broth (page 237) or water
2 teaspoons fish sauce
sea salt and freshly ground black pepper
1 large handful of coriander leaves
1 lime, cut into wedges

See Glossary

❶ Melt 2 tablespoons of the oil or fat in a wok or large frying pan over medium–high heat. Add the prawns in batches and cook for 30–60 seconds on each side until lightly golden but still raw in the centre. Remove the prawns from the pan and set aside.

❷ Reduce the heat to medium and add the remaining oil to the pan, along with the shallot, garlic and chilli. Cook, stirring frequently, for 2 minutes.

❸ Mix the turmeric and ground coriander into the shallot mixture and cook for 30 seconds until fragrant. Add the diced tomatoes, broth or water and fish sauce and simmer for 5 minutes. Return the prawns to the pan and cook for 2 minutes until the prawns are almost cooked through. Remove from the heat and adjust the seasoning with some extra fish sauce or salt and pepper.

❹ Divide the curry between serving plates, scatter on the coriander and serve with the lime wedges on the side, to squeeze over the top.

If you can find a wild-caught salmon and are catering for a crowd, I recommend you cook it as I have done here. There are few things that can be compared to a perfectly cooked salmon, perfumed with fresh herbs and lemon. I have teamed the salmon with a delicious sweet potato and egg salad that is sure to make your guests extremely happy. Toss through some fermented veg and you will be laughing.

Whole Roasted SALMON
WITH LEMON AND HERBS
SERVES 6

1 small handful of thyme leaves

1 small handful of oregano leaves

1 lemon, thickly sliced

8 garlic cloves, halved

1 × 3 kg whole salmon, cleaned, scaled and gutted

sea salt and freshly ground black pepper

2 tablespoons coconut oil or good-quality animal fat*, melted

Sweet potato, egg and watercress salad

2 sweet potatoes, cut into 2 cm cubes

2 tablespoons apple cider vinegar

4 tablespoons extra-virgin olive oil

1 garlic clove, crushed

sea salt and freshly ground black pepper

2 large handfuls of watercress or mesclun leaves

½ fennel bulb, very thinly sliced

3 hard-boiled eggs, peeled and crumbled

* See Glossary

① Preheat the oven to 180°C. Line a large baking tray with baking paper and scatter one-third of the thyme, oregano, lemon and garlic across it.

② Place the fish on top of the herbs and lemon and fill its cavity with the remaining herbs, lemon and garlic. Season well with salt and pepper.

③ Drizzle the oil or fat over the fish and roast in the oven for 50 minutes. To check if the fish is cooked, insert a metal skewer into the thickest part of the flesh. Hold the skewer there for 10 seconds, then pull it out and lightly touch it to the inside of your wrist. If the skewer feels hot, the fish is cooked. If it is only warm, the fish should be cooked for another 10–15 minutes before re-checking.

④ To make the salad, place the sweet potato in a saucepan of salted water and bring to a simmer. Cook until tender, about 15 minutes, then drain. Mix the vinegar, oil, garlic, 1 tablespoon of water and some salt and pepper in a bowl. Combine the sweet potato, watercress or mesclun, fennel and egg in a large bowl, drizzle on the dressing and lightly toss.

⑤ Serve the salmon with the salad.

Jimmy Shu owns Hanuman in Darwin, one of my favourite restaurants in Australia, and showcases Indian, Sri Lankan, Malaysian and Nonya cuisines – demonstrating his affinity with his own heritage. My go-to dish is the barramundi meen moolie, which is luscious, creamy and full of flavour. The good news is it is very easy to make at home. If you are ever near one of Jimmy's restaurants, pop in and say hi.

Hanuman COCONUT-INFUSED
BARRAMUNDI

SERVES 2–4

600 g barramundi fillets, skin
   removed, cut into 3 cm pieces
sea salt
2 tablespoons coconut oil or
   good-quality animal fat*
1 large red onion, sliced
2 lemongrass stalks, white part
   only, bruised with the back
   of a knife and cut in half
   lengthways
5 cm piece of ginger, sliced
1 long red chilli, deseeded and finely
   sliced
28 fresh curry leaves (about
   2 sprigs)
600 ml coconut cream
1½ teaspoons ground turmeric
350 ml Fish Bone Broth (page 237)
200 g tomatoes, cut into wedges
1 teaspoon coconut sugar (optional)
freshly ground black pepper
coriander leaves, to serve
Cauliflower Rice (page 233), to serve

* See Glossary

❶ Season the fish with a touch of salt.

❷ Heat the oil or fat in a deep, heavy-based frying pan over medium heat, add the onion, lemongrass, ginger, chilli and curry leaves and stir-fry for 5 minutes until soft.

❸ Add the coconut cream and turmeric to the pan and bring to the boil. Reduce the heat to low, pour in the broth, then stir in the tomato. Add the sugar (if using) and season with salt and pepper.

❹ Gently add the fish pieces to the pan and poach in the coconut broth for 8 minutes until cooked through. Scatter on the coriander leaves and serve immediately with the cauliflower rice on the side.

Tagines are popular in Moroccan cuisine and are named after the dish they are traditionally cooked in. Out of all the one pot wonders, tagines have to be in my top five, as they keep me coming back for more. You can use pretty much any fish or crustacean – or try poultry or lamb – here and still create a culinary masterpiece, as the base flavours and cooking techniques guarantee a killer dish every time.

SERVES 4

Mackerel TAGINE

2 tablespoons coconut oil

1 onion, chopped

2.5 cm piece of ginger, finely grated

3 garlic cloves, finely chopped

1–2 long red chillies, deseeded and sliced

2 tomatoes, chopped

50 g pitted black olives, halved

½ head of cauliflower (about 400 g), broken into bite-sized florets

250 ml (1 cup) Fish or Chicken Bone Broth (pages 237 and 234)

16 fresh okra pods*

700 g mackerel fillets, skin on, cut into 3 cm pieces (or use white-fleshed fish fillets or whole sardines)

sea salt and freshly ground black pepper

2 large handfuls of baby spinach

coriander leaves, to serve

lime wedges, to serve

Spice mix

1 tablespoon paprika

1 teaspoon ground turmeric

1 teaspoon ground allspice

1½ teaspoons ground coriander

½ teaspoon cassia bark*

½ teaspoon ground cardamom

1 teaspoon chilli flakes

See Glossary

❶ To make the spice mix, combine all the ingredients in a bowl. You need only 1 tablespoon of spice mix for this recipe, so store the leftover mix in an airtight container in the pantry for up to 6 months.

❷ Heat the oil in a frying pan or tagine over medium heat. Add the onion and cook, stirring occasionally, for 5–8 minutes or until translucent. Stir in 1 tablespoon of the spice mix and cook, stirring constantly, for 30 seconds until fragrant. Add the ginger, garlic and chilli and cook for 1 minute until softened. Add the tomato, olives and cauliflower, then pour in the broth and bring to the boil. Cover, reduce the heat to low and simmer for 5 minutes.

❸ Add the okra and fish, season with salt and pepper, cover with a lid and cook for 7 minutes until the fish is cooked through. Remove from the heat and fold through the spinach.

❹ To finish, scatter on the coriander leaves and serve with the lime wedges.

Chapter Three
POULTRY

It is said the phrase 'winner winner chicken dinner' originates from 1970s casinos that were trying to attract players to underplayed tables. At the time, the most common bet was $2. Coincidentally, most casinos offered a chicken dinner for just under $2. Dealers would call out 'Winner winner chicken dinner' when someone won the equivalent of a chicken dinner. How funny then that this dish costs about $2 per person and is one of the healthiest dishes in the world.

Chicken and Vegetable COMFORT SOUP

SERVES 6–8

2 tablespoons coconut oil or
    good-quality animal fat*
1 onion, chopped
3 garlic cloves, finely chopped
1 large carrot, chopped
1 celery stalk, halved lengthways
    and cut into 1 cm thick slices
4 thyme sprigs
1 bay leaf
1.75 litres (7 cups) Chicken Bone
    Broth (page 234), plus extra
    if needed
1 tablespoon finely grated ginger
1 zucchini, cut into 2 cm cubes
500 g kent pumpkin, cut into
    2 cm cubes
450 g shredded poached chicken
200 g silverbeet, shredded
sea salt and freshly ground
    black pepper
1 handful of flat-leaf parsley leaves,
    finely chopped

* See Glossary

❶ Melt the oil or fat in a stockpot over medium heat. Add the onion, garlic, carrot, celery, thyme and bay leaf. Cook, stirring occasionally, for 6 minutes until the vegetables are soft but not browned.

❷ Pour the broth into the pot and bring to the boil, then reduce the heat to low and simmer for 20 minutes.

❸ Add the ginger, zucchini and pumpkin to the pot and cook for a further 15 minutes until the pumpkin is tender. Add the chicken and silverbeet and simmer for another few minutes until the silverbeet is cooked.

❹ Season the soup with salt and pepper and sprinkle on the parsley before serving.

PRESSURE COOKER Follow step ❶, using your pressure cooker over medium heat. Add the broth, ginger, zucchini, pumpkin and silverbeet, then bring the cooker to high pressure and cook over medium heat for 5 minutes. Let the pressure drop naturally before opening the lid. Stir through the chicken and leave to sit for a few minutes until heated through. Follow step ❹.

SLOW COOKER Follow step ❶, using a frying pan. Transfer the sautéed vegetables to your slow cooker, pour in the broth, cover with the lid and cook on low for 6 hours. Add the ginger, zucchini, pumpkin and silverbeet, cover with the lid and cook on low for 3 hours until the vegetables are tender. Stir in the chicken and cook for a further 5 minutes until heated through. Follow step ❹.

One of my favourite dishes in the world for its sheer simplicity is the classic congee. I think this congee could become your new favourite all-time breakfast, as it is so quick to make. If time is an issue, you can make it the night before and reheat it in the morning.

SERVES 4

CONGEE, *My Way*

600 g cauliflower florets

1 litre (4 cups) Chicken Bone Broth (page 234)

2.5 cm piece of ginger, finely sliced

250 g leftover roast chicken, shredded

1 handful of coriander leaves, roughly chopped

2 spring onions, white and green part, finely sliced

1–2 long red chillies, finely sliced

2 tablespoons tamari or coconut aminos*

sea salt and freshly ground white pepper

4 eggs

To serve

toasted sesame seeds

sesame oil

coriander leaves

kimchi (for a recipe, see page 238)

* See Glossary

❶ Place the cauliflower in the bowl of a food processor and pulse into tiny pieces that resemble rice.

❷ Combine the cauliflower rice, broth and ginger in a large saucepan and bring to the boil.

❸ Reduce the heat to medium, cover and simmer for 30 minutes until the congee is lovely and soupy. Add more broth if needed.

❹ Add the chicken, chopped coriander, spring onion, chilli and tamari or coconut aminos to the congee and season with salt and pepper. Return to a simmer and cook for 2 minutes.

❺ Divide the congee among four bowls and crack an egg into the centre of each one. Allow to stand for 3–5 minutes so the heat from the congee cooks the egg. Sprinkle on the sesame seeds, drizzle with the sesame oil and scatter on the coriander leaves. Serve with the kimchi on the side.

PRESSURE COOKER Follow step ❶. Follow step ❷, using your pressure cooker. Close the lid and lock it, then bring the cooker to high pressure and cook over medium heat for 5 minutes. Let the pressure drop naturally before opening the lid. Increase the heat to high and follow step ❹ to finish cooking. Follow step ❺.

SLOW COOKER Follow step ❶. Using your slow cooker, follow step ❷. Cover with the lid and cook on high for 2 hours until the cauliflower is soft. Follow step ❹, cover and cook on high for 5 minutes. Follow step ❺.

Ginger has been used for centuries to aid digestion, help with nausea, morning sickness and travel sickness, and reduce muscle stiffness and pain. I love playing around with it in the kitchen, as it works wonders in so many dishes, from savoury to sweet. I particularly love the flavour it brings to poultry dishes. Here is a wonderful warming dish for the whole family. I have cut a whole chook into pieces but feel free to use thighs (with the skin on), drumsticks or marylands.

SERVES 4–6

Braised GINGER CHICKEN

1 × 1.8 kg chicken, cut into 8 pieces

1 tablespoon tapioca flour*
(optional)

3 tablespoons coconut oil or
good-quality animal fat*, melted

1 onion, chopped

4 garlic cloves, finely sliced

5 cm piece of ginger, cut into
thin strips

sea salt and freshly ground
black pepper

125 ml (½ cup) dry white wine

250 ml (1 cup) Chicken Bone Broth
(page 234)

1 tablespoon fish sauce

1 tablespoon tamari or coconut
aminos*

3 long red chillies, deseeded and
finely sliced (leave some seeds in
if you like it spicy)

4 spring onions, cut into thin strips

1 bunch of bok choy (about 300 g),
trimmed

lightly toasted sesame seeds,
to serve

See Glossary

1 Preheat the oven to 160°C.

2 Place the chicken pieces in a large bowl, add the tapioca flour (if using) and toss to coat.

3 Melt the oil or fat in a roasting tin over medium–high heat. Add the onion and cook, stirring occasionally, for 5 minutes until translucent. Stir in the garlic and ginger and cook for 1 minute until fragrant. Add the chicken pieces, skin-side down, season with salt and pepper and cook for 3 minutes until lightly golden.

4 Pour in the wine, broth, fish sauce and tamari or coconut aminos and scatter over the chilli and spring onion.

5 Cover tightly with a double layer of foil and braise in the oven for 45 minutes.

6 Remove the chicken from the oven and mix in the bok choy. Cover and return to the oven for 15 minutes until the chicken is cooked through.

7 Season the sauce if needed. Sprinkle the sesame seeds over the braised chicken and serve with a side of Asian greens.

PRESSURE COOKER Follow steps **2**–**3**, using your pressure cooker over medium heat. Follow step **4**, but add only 170 ml of broth rather than 250 ml. Close the lid and lock it, then bring the cooker to high pressure over high heat. Reduce the heat to medium and cook for 15 minutes. Let the pressure drop naturally before opening the lid. Add the bok choy and cook over high heat for a further 5 minutes until the bok choy is tender. Follow step **7**.

SLOW COOKER Follow step **2**. Using a large frying pan, follow step **3**. Transfer the chicken and vegetables to your slow cooker. Follow step **4**, but add only 170 ml of broth rather than 250 ml. Cover and cook on low for 6–7 hours. Stir through the bok choy, cover and cook on high for another 15 minutes until the chicken and bok choy are cooked through. Follow step **7**.

The number one piece of advice I can give about going paleo is to be prepared, so you always have delicious nutrient-dense meals on hand. If you cook in bulk – and double or triple recipes – you will always have food in the fridge or freezer ready to go when you need a quick meal. And that is where this recipe works perfectly – you can double or triple it with ease, and it tastes better the next day. Serve with cauliflower or broccoli rice or a side of vegetables or salad.

Chinese CLAYPOT *Chicken*

SERVES 4–6

2 tablespoons coconut oil or good-quality animal fat*

4 chicken marylands (about 1.2 kg), drumstick and thigh separated

sea salt and freshly ground black pepper

200 g fresh shiitake mushrooms, halved

2 slices of rindless bacon, cut into thin strips

1 tablespoon tamari or coconut aminos*

375 ml (1½ cups) Chicken Bone Broth (page 234)

2 teaspoons honey

5 garlic cloves, finely chopped

4 spring onions, cut on the diagonal into 3 cm batons

2.5 cm piece of ginger, cut into thin strips

pinch of chilli powder

1 long red chilli, deseeded and halved lengthways

300 g Chinese broccoli (gai larn), chopped in half

* See Glossary

1 Place the oil or fat in a claypot or flameproof casserole dish over medium–high heat. Season the chicken with salt and pepper, then cook for 2–3 minutes on each side until lightly golden. Stir through the mushrooms, bacon, tamari or coconut aminos, broth, honey, garlic, spring onion, ginger, chilli powder and chilli and bring to the boil.

2 Reduce the heat to low, cover with a lid and simmer for 40 minutes until the chicken is cooked through.

3 Add the Chinese broccoli to the pot, cover and cook for 10 minutes until it is cooked through.

PRESSURE COOKER Follow step **1** using a pressure cooker over medium–high heat. Close and lock the lid, then bring the cooker to high pressure and cook over medium heat for 15 minutes. Release the pressure naturally before opening the lid. Add the Chinese broccoli, close and lock the lid, then bring the cooker to high pressure and cook for 2 minutes. Let the pressure drop naturally before opening the lid and serving.

SLOW COOKER Follow step **1** using a large saucepan. Transfer the chicken and vegetables to your slow cooker. Cover and cook on high for 4 hours. Mix in the Chinese broccoli, cover and cook for a further 20 minutes, then serve.

I remember when I was an eager young chef trying to make my mark on the Australian culinary landscape. I prepared master stock in my restaurants and loved the flavour it imparted on a gently poached piece of meat. Make sure you save and reuse your master stock – each time you cook the stock the flavour intensifies and it tastes even better!

POACHED CHICKEN
SERVES 4–6 *in Master Stock*

1 × 1.8 kg chicken
Cauliflower Rice (page 233), to serve

Master stock
2.4 litres Chicken Bone Broth
   (page 234) or water
200 ml tamari or coconut aminos*
100 g coconut sugar or honey
   (optional)
5 cm piece of ginger, sliced
3 cinnamon sticks
3 green cardamom pods, crushed
   (optional)
4 garlic cloves, roughly chopped
1 long red chilli, roughly chopped
4 pieces of dried mandarin or
   orange zest
1 spring onion, white part only,
   roughly chopped
3 star anise
2 teaspoons Sichuan peppercorns
1 teaspoon sea salt
1 small handful of coriander roots,
   washed well

* See Glossary

❶ To make the master stock, place all the ingredients in a stockpot over medium–high heat, bring to the boil, then reduce the heat to low and simmer for 30 minutes.

❷ Bring the stock back to the boil, add the chicken, reduce the heat to medium–low and simmer for 10 minutes.

❸ Turn off the heat, cover the pot with a lid and allow to stand for 1½ hours until the chicken is cooked through.

❹ Chop the chicken into pieces and serve with steamed Asian greens and the cauliflower rice.

PRESSURE COOKER Using your pressure cooker over medium–high heat, follow step ❶. Add the chicken and check the level of the master stock in your pressure cooker. If the cooker is more than two-thirds full, ladle out some of the stock. Close the lid and lock it, then bring the cooker to high pressure and cook over medium heat for 35 minutes. Let the pressure drop naturally before opening the lid. Follow step ❹.

SLOW COOKER Follow step ❶. Transfer the master stock to your slow cooker. Add the chicken, cover with the lid and cook on low for 8–10 hours until the chicken is cooked through. Follow step ❹.

Tip Reserve the master stock for other recipes. Simply strain, bring to the boil, then cool and store in the fridge for 1 week or the freezer for up to 6 months. It is fantastic for poaching meat, fish and vegetables.

This really is a meal the whole family will enjoy. I have made it paleo friendly by replacing the grains with ground almonds. If you are avoiding nuts, then use sunflower or pumpkin seed flour or coconut flour. To make this dish sing, the key is to use a top-quality full-flavoured broth. Then it is up to you how simple or fancy you make it. I have used kelp noodles, but you could use carrot, pumpkin, parsnip, swede or zucchini noodles instead.

SERVES 4

Jewish PENICILLIN

2 tablespoons coconut oil or
   good-quality animal fat*
1 onion, chopped
3 garlic cloves, crushed
1 large carrot, chopped
2 celery stalks, halved lengthways
   and cut into 1 cm chunks
150 g green cabbage, shredded
4 thyme sprigs
1 bay leaf
1.25 litres (5 cups) Chicken Bone
   Broth (page 234)
200 g kelp noodles*, roughly chopped
300 g (1½ cups) finely shredded
   leftover cooked chicken
sea salt and freshly ground
   black pepper
1 small handful of dill fronds
lemon wedges, to serve

Paleo 'matzo' balls
4 eggs
3 tablespoons coconut oil or
   good-quality animal fat*
1 teaspoon sea salt
¼ teaspoon freshly ground
   black pepper
155 g (1½ cups) almond meal
3 tablespoons psyllium husks*

* See Glossary

❶ To make the paleo matzo balls, whisk the eggs in a bowl, then add the remaining ingredients and mix with a wooden spoon to form a very thick doughy paste. Cover with plastic wrap and place in the fridge for 30 minutes for the dough to harden slightly. Wet your hands with cold water and shape the chilled dough into 20 bite-sized balls. (Don't make the balls too large as they will double in size when cooking.) Set aside.

❷ Melt the oil or fat in a large saucepan over medium heat. Add the onion, garlic, carrot, celery, cabbage, thyme and bay leaf and cook, stirring regularly, for 6 minutes until the vegetables are soft. Pour in the broth and bring to the boil.

❸ Reduce the heat to low and simmer the soup for 20 minutes.

❹ Add the matzo balls and noodles to the soup.

❺ Cover and simmer for 5 minutes until the balls float to the top. Stir in the chicken and simmer for a few more minutes until heated through.

❻ Season with salt and pepper, sprinkle on the dill and serve with lemon wedges on the side.

PRESSURE COOKER Follow step ❶. Using your pressure cooker over medium heat, follow step ❷. Close the lid and lock it, then bring the cooker to high pressure and cook over medium heat for 5 minutes. Naturally release the pressure before opening the lid. Follow step ❹, add the chicken and cook, uncovered, over medium heat until the matzo balls float to the top and the chicken is heated through. Follow step ❻.

SLOW COOKER Follow steps ❶–❷, then transfer all the ingredients from the saucepan to your slow cooker. Cover and cook on low for 6 hours. Add the matzo balls, noodles and chicken to the soup, cover and cook on high for 1 hour. Follow step ❻.

You don't need to be a rocket scientist to know that the list of ingredients for this dish scream good health. Now, a lot of people may be put off by this many ingredients in a recipe, but I get excited about the adventure that is about to happen in my kitchen – and later on my tastebuds. This curry may take a little while to prepare, but if you make a big batch, you will have meals for days to come. Serve with a refreshing cucumber and lettuce salad and some fermented veg.

SERVES 4–6

Duck VINDALOO

1¼ tablespoons duck fat or other good-quality animal fat, melted
3 tablespoons apple cider vinegar
6 duck legs (about 1.2 kg)
sea salt and freshly ground black pepper
8 red Asian shallots, quartered lengthways
6 garlic cloves, finely chopped
1½ tablespoons finely grated ginger
3 tomatoes, chopped
1 bay leaf
500 ml (2 cups) Chicken Bone Broth (page 234)
2 bunches of broccolini, roughly chopped into large pieces
1 large handful of baby spinach
½ teaspoon dried chilli flakes (or more if you like it spicy)

Spice paste
6 long red chillies, deseeded and roughly chopped
1½ teaspoons cumin seeds
1 teaspoon brown or yellow mustard seeds
1 teaspoon fenugreek seeds
4 green cardamom pods, bruised
1 teaspoon ground allspice
1½ teaspoons ground turmeric
2 tablespoons tomato paste

1 Preheat the oven to 160°C.

2 To make the spice paste, combine all the ingredients in the bowl of a food processor and whiz to a fine paste. Heat 1 teaspoon of the fat in a large frying pan over medium–low heat. Add the spice paste and cook, stirring frequently, for 30 seconds until fragrant. Transfer to a bowl, mix in the vinegar and set aside.

3 Coat the duck legs with the remaining fat and season with salt and pepper. Increase the heat to medium–high. Working in batches, add the duck, skin-side down, to the pan. Cook for 4–5 minutes until the skin is golden and crisp, then flip over and cook for 2 minutes. Transfer the duck to a plate. Drain most of the fat from the pan, leaving only 2 tablespoons. (The leftover fat can be stored in the fridge for up to 2 weeks and used for all kinds of cooking.)

4 Reduce the heat to medium, add the shallot to the pan and cook, stirring occasionally, for 8 minutes until translucent. Add the garlic, ginger and tomato and cook, stirring occasionally, for 5 minutes until the tomato has broken down. Add the spice paste, bay leaf and broth, bring to the boil, then return the duck to the pan.

5 Reduce the heat to low, cover and cook in the oven for 1½ hours. Remove the lid, increase the temperature to 180°C and cook for a further 30 minutes. Add the broccolini to the curry 5 minutes before it is ready. Season with salt and pepper, stir in the spinach and chilli and serve.

PRESSURE COOKER Follow steps **2**–**3** using your pressure cooker. Increase the heat to medium–high and follow step **4**, but add only 350 ml of broth rather than 500 ml. Close the lid and lock it, then bring to high pressure and cook over medium heat for 50 minutes. Let the pressure drop naturally before opening the lid. Add the broccolini and cook, uncovered, for 5 minutes. Season and stir in the spinach and chilli.

SLOW COOKER Follow steps **2**–**4**, but add only 380 ml of broth rather than 500 ml. Transfer all the ingredients to your slow cooker, cover and cook on low for 10 hours until the duck is tender. Add the broccolini and cook, uncovered, on high for 30 minutes. Season and stir in the spinach and chilli.

This is the type of food I dream of eating. When simmered long and slow, the cinnamon, cumin and star anise bring an element of warmth and comfort to this dish – as well as to the kitchen. The dates add a little sweetness, but you could just as easily use sultanas, currants or goji berries. Cook double the amount, as you will want leftovers to enjoy the next day. Great served with some fermented veg on the side.

Spiced CHICKEN with CHORIZO and DATES

SERVES 4

4 chicken marylands (about 1.2 kg)

sea salt and freshly ground
   black pepper

2½ tablespoons good-quality
   animal fat*

1 chorizo sausage (about 150 g),
   thickly sliced

2 red onions, sliced

4 garlic cloves, sliced

1–2 long red or green chillies,
   deseeded and chopped (leave
   the seeds in if you like it spicy)

1 teaspoon ground cumin

¾ teaspoon ground cinnamon

½ red capsicum, cut into
   2 cm strips

½ green capsicum, cut into
   2 cm strips

2 tomatoes, diced

600 ml Chicken Bone Broth
   (page 234)

2 cinnamon sticks

2 star anise

4 medjool dates, pitted and cut
   into quarters

1 handful of coriander leaves,
   to serve

* See Glossary

1 Preheat the oven to 180°C.

2 Season the chicken with salt and pepper.

3 Melt half the fat in a large flameproof casserole dish over medium–high heat and add the chicken in batches. Cook for 2–3 minutes on each side until golden, then remove from the dish.

4 Add the chorizo to the dish and cook on each side for 30 seconds until golden and crisp. Remove from the dish.

5 Reduce the heat to medium and melt the remaining fat in the dish. Add the onion and sauté for 5 minutes until translucent. Add the garlic, chilli, cumin and ground cinnamon and fry for 30 seconds until fragrant. Stir in the red and green capsicum and 3 tablespoons of water and cook for 2 minutes until softened.

6 Add the tomato to the dish, pour in the broth and stir in the cinnamon sticks and star anise. Return the chicken and chorizo to the dish, add the dates and bring to the boil.

7 Cover the dish with a tight-fitting lid and transfer to the oven. Cook for 35 minutes, then remove the lid and cook for a further 20 minutes until the chicken is cooked through.

8 Season to taste, divide among four serving bowls, scatter on the coriander leaves and serve.

PRESSURE COOKER Follow step **2**. Using your pressure cooker over medium–high heat, follow steps **3**–**6**, adding only 420 ml of broth rather than 600 ml. Close and lock the lid, then bring the cooker to high pressure over high heat. Reduce the heat to medium and cook for 15 minutes. Let the pressure drop naturally before opening the lid. Follow step **8**.

SLOW COOKER Follow steps **2**–**5**, then transfer all the ingredients from the casserole dish to your slow cooker. Follow step **6**, but add only 420 ml of stock rather than 600 ml. Cover and cook on low for 6–8 hours until the chicken is cooked through. Follow step **8**.

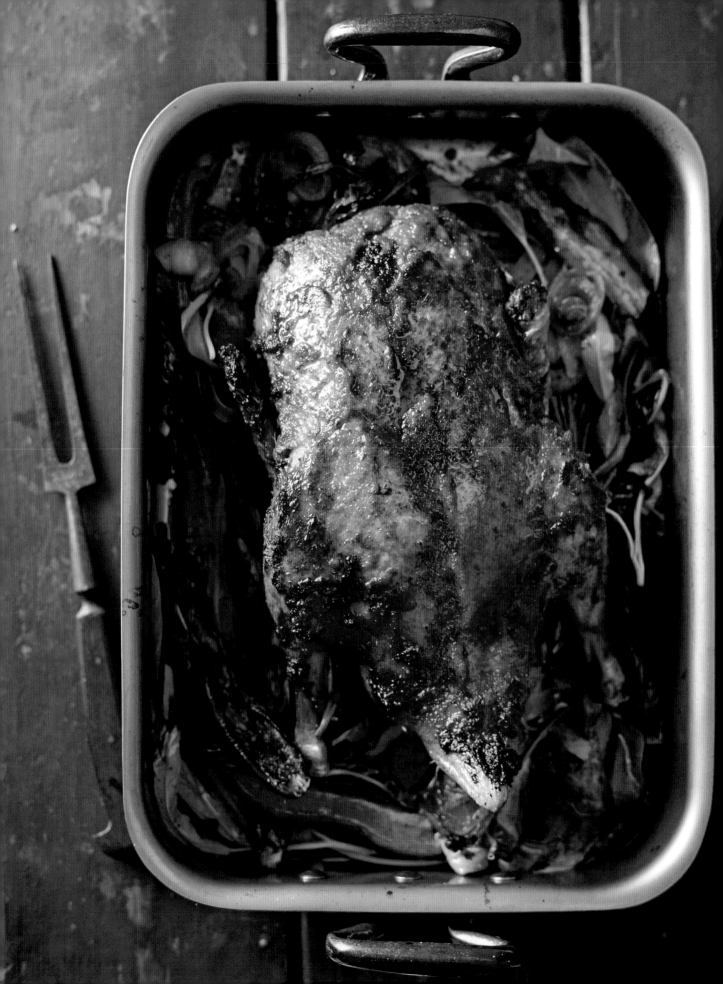

In my travels to Indonesia I have discovered that many of the local dishes are paleo by default – with animal protein serving as the backdrop to an array of amazing vegetables and broths. Here, we take the classic roast and, to tantalise the tastebuds, give it some Indonesian love. If duck is a little hard to come by, simply swap it for chook, pork belly or marinated barbecued lamb chops. Serve with loads of veg or salad and some fermented veg on the side.

SERVES 4

Balinese ROAST DUCK

1 × 2.2 kg duck

2 teaspoons sea salt

2 tablespoons coconut oil or good-quality animal fat*

1 lime, cut in half

500 ml (2 cups) Chicken Bone Broth (page 234)

4 French shallots, cut into wedges

8 fresh curry leaves

1 large sweet potato, cut into wedges

5 Japanese eggplants, green tips removed and halved lengthways

freshly ground black pepper

2 large handfuls of water spinach*

Spice paste

8 macadamia nuts

3 French shallots, roughly chopped

7 long red chillies, deseeded and roughly chopped

3 tablespoons finely chopped galangal*

3 tablespoons finely chopped ginger

1½ tablespoons finely chopped fresh turmeric (or 1½ teaspoons ground turmeric)

2 tablespoons tamarind puree*

1½ teaspoons shrimp paste

1 tablespoon tamari or coconut aminos*

2 tablespoons honey

1 teaspoon sea salt

2 tablespoons coconut oil

* See Glossary

❶ Preheat the oven to 120ºC.

❷ Place the duck in a large roasting tin and rub the salt and oil or fat over the duck to evenly coat. Set aside.

❸ To make the spice paste, place all the ingredients and 3 tablespoons of water in the bowl of a food processor and whiz to a fine paste.

❹ Rub the spice paste evenly on the skin and in the cavity of the duck, then stuff the lime into the cavity. Pour the broth into the tin, scatter around the shallot and curry leaves and tightly cover with foil. Roast in the oven for 5 hours until the duck is cooked through.

❺ Increase the oven temperature to 200ºC. Remove the foil, add the sweet potato and eggplant to the tin and season the vegetables with salt and pepper. Return to the oven to roast, basting the duck with the juices in the tin, for 30 minutes until the vegetables are cooked through and the duck is golden. Mix in the spinach and serve.

Tip If you can't get your hands on water spinach, use baby spinach leaves instead.

I love creating memorable dishes that are full of wonderful aromatic spices and herbs that permeate not only our senses but also our kitchens and homes. Here is a lovely Persian dish that uses walnuts, pomegranate and delightful spices to turn the humble chicken into a culinary masterpiece that won't be easily forgotten.

Persian CHICKEN STEW *with Pomegranate*

SERVES 4–6

100 g (1 cup) walnuts (activated
    if possible*), toasted
3 tablespoons coconut oil
1 kg chicken thigh fillets, cut into
    2 cm pieces
sea salt and freshly ground
    black pepper
1 large onion, chopped
2 garlic cloves, chopped
1 teaspoon ground turmeric
½ teaspoon ground cinnamon
¼ teaspoon freshly grated nutmeg
2 pinches of saffron
600 ml Chicken Bone Broth
    (page 234)
1 tablespoon pomegranate
    molasses*
1 tablespoon coconut sugar
    (optional)

To serve
seeds of ¼ pomegranate
mint leaves
sumac*
Cauliflower Rice (page 233)

* See Glossary

① Place the walnuts in the bowl of a food possessor and whiz until coarsley ground. Set aside.

② Melt 2 tablespoons of the oil in a large frying pan over medium–high heat. Add the chicken in batches, season with salt and pepper and cook for 2 minutes on all sides until golden, then remove from the pan.

③ Melt the remaining oil in the pan over medium heat, add the onion and sauté until translucent, about 5–6 minutes. Add the garlic and cook for 1 minute until soft. Add the spices and cook for a further 30 seconds.

④ Return the chicken pieces to the pan, then pour in the broth.

⑤ Bring to the boil, reduce the heat to low, cover and simmer gently for 30 minutes.

⑥ Stir in the walnuts, pomegranate molasses and sugar (if using). For a stronger sweet and sour flavour, add another tablespoon each of molasses and sugar.

⑦ Continue to cook, stirring occasionally, for 1 hour until the chicken is tender and the sauce has thickened.

⑧ Season the stew with salt and pepper, scatter on some pomegranate seeds, mint leaves and sumac and serve with the cauliflower rice on the side.

PRESSURE COOKER Follow step ①. Using your pressure cooker over medium–high heat, follow steps ②–④, but add only 420 ml of broth rather than 600 ml. Close the lid and lock it, then bring to high pressure and cook over medium heat for 10 minutes. Use the quick release method to open the lid (see page 11). Follow step ⑥, close and lock the lid, then bring to high pressure and cook over medium heat for 5 minutes. Let the pressure drop naturally before opening the lid. Follow step ⑧.

SLOW COOKER Follow steps ①–③, then transfer the chicken, 420 ml of broth and all the ingredients in the pan to your slow cooker. Cover and cook on low for 6 hours. Follow step ⑥ and cook, uncovered, on high for 1 hour until the sauce has reduced slightly and the chicken is cooked through. Follow step ⑧.

Sometimes we crave something simple and familiar – and this is where a classic roast chicken comes in! You know that everyone in the family will love this dish – it isn't heavily spiced and doesn't have any unfamiliar ingredients. If you are adopting a paleo lifestyle, start slowly and try not to stress your family with a new routine. Simply cook beautiful food they can't resist and don't tell them they are eating paleo.

ROAST CHICKEN *with* GARLIC *and* THYME

SERVES 4–6

2 garlic bulbs, halved horizontally
1 handful of thyme sprigs
1 parsnip, thickly sliced lengthways
1 onion, unpeeled, thickly sliced
1 carrot, thickly sliced lengthways
1 lemon, cut in half
1 × 1.8 kg chicken
3 tablespoons coconut oil or
   good-quality animal fat*, melted
sea salt and freshly ground
   black pepper
200 ml Chicken Bone Broth
   (page 234) or water

* See Glossary

① Preheat the oven to 200ºC.

② Scatter the garlic and thyme in the base of a large roasting tin, then add the parsnip, onion, carrot and lemon.

③ Rinse the chicken inside and out, pat dry with paper towel, rub with the oil or fat and season generously with salt and pepper. Place in the tin and pour in the broth or water.

④ Transfer to the oven and roast the chicken, basting occasionally with the juices in the tin, for 30 minutes. Reduce the temperature to 170ºC and cook for a further 30–45 minutes until golden and the juices run clear when the thigh is pierced with a skewer.

⑤ Remove the chicken from the oven, cover with foil and rest in a warm place for 10 minutes.

⑥ Carve the chicken and serve with the roasted vegetables.

Tip Roast two chooks so that you have heaps of leftover meat for salads, stir-fries and soups.

I love one pot cooking because it is so easy to make a lot and then pop the leftovers into containers for breakfast or lunch over the next few days. Give this recipe a try if you have never eaten Ethiopian food. I guarantee it will become a firm family favourite. Oh, and add some green veg – like broccoli, spinach, kale or silverbeet – at the end of cooking, or serve with a big salad and a side of fermented veg.

Ethiopian RED Chicken STEW

SERVES 4

2 tablespoons coconut oil or
    good-quality animal fat*, melted
1.5 kg onions, finely chopped
6 garlic cloves, finely chopped
1 tablespoon finely grated ginger
4 tablespoons apple cider vinegar
juice of 1 lemon
6 chicken marylands, drumstick
    and thigh separated
sea salt
1 cinnamon stick
250 ml (1 cup) Chicken Bone Broth
    (page 234)
8 hard-boiled eggs, peeled

Spice mix
2½ tablespoons paprika
¼ teaspoon ground allspice
¼ teaspoon freshly grated nutmeg
½ teaspoon ground coriander
½ teaspoon fenugreek
15 green cardamom pods
1 tablespoon nigella seeds
1 tablespoon fennel seeds
1 teaspoon dried basil
1 teaspoon black peppercorns

See Glossary

❶ To make the spice mix, combine the spices and grind to a fine powder in a spice grinder or using a mortar and pestle. Set aside.

❷ Heat the oil or fat in a large saucepan over low heat and add the onion, garlic and ginger.

❸ Cover the pan with the lid and cook, stirring occasionally, for 30 minutes until the onion is caramelised.

❹ Meanwhile, mix the vinegar and lemon juice in a bowl, add the chicken, cover and marinate in the fridge for 20 minutes. Drain, discarding the liquid.

❺ Stir the ground spices and the cinnamon stick into the onion mixture. Add the chicken pieces, pour in the broth and season with a little salt.

❻ Reduce the heat to low, cover the pan and simmer the stew for 1 hour until the chicken is cooked through.

❼ Add the eggs to the stew, then spoon into shallow bowls and serve.

PRESSURE COOKER Follow step ❶. Using your pressure cooker, follow step ❷ and add 3 tablespoons of water. Close the lid and lock it, then bring the cooker to high pressure and cook over medium heat for 10 minutes. Use the quick release method to open the lid (see page 11). Follow steps ❹–❺, but add only 180 ml of broth rather than 250 ml. Close the lid and lock it, then bring the cooker to high pressure and cook over medium heat for 30 minutes. Let the pressure drop naturally before opening the lid. Cook, uncovered, over medium heat for 10 minutes to reduce the sauce. Follow step ❼.

SLOW COOKER Follow steps ❶–❸, then transfer all the ingredients from the saucepan to your slow cooker. Follow steps ❹–❺, but add only 180 ml of broth rather than 250 ml. Cover and cook on low for 8–10 hours. Follow step ❼.

This is a nod to my traditional French culinary roots, which have a lot in common with paleo cooking. As a chef and health coach, I find it fascinating that my two lives have intertwined and I can demonstrate the art of healthy eating through a dish like this cassoulet. This meal has everything – healing bone broth, good-quality saturated fat and protein, and pigment-rich vegetables. Make sure you serve your cassoulet with some green veggies and a spoon of fermented veg.

SERVES 4–6

Duck CASSOULET

4 confit duck legs (for a recipe, see page 112)

sea salt and freshly ground black pepper

3 tablespoons duck fat or other good-quality animal fat*

1 onion, finely chopped

1 carrot, finely chopped

1 celery stalk, diced

1 long red chilli, deseeded and finely chopped

150 g pancetta, diced

4 garlic cloves, chopped

1 tomato, chopped

1 small ham hock (about 800 g)

2 bay leaves

a few thyme sprigs

1 litre (4 cups) Chicken Bone Broth (page 234)

2 parsnips, cut into 1 cm cubes

1 large sweet potato, cut into 1 cm cubes

1 swede, cut into 1 cm cubes

3 paleo pork and garlic sausages

finely chopped flat-leaf parsley leaves, to serve

* See Glossary

1 Preheat the oven to 160°C.

2 Season the duck legs with salt and pepper. Melt the fat in a flameproof casserole dish over medium–high heat. Add the duck legs and cook for 2 minutes on each side until golden and crisp, then remove from the dish.

3 Add the onion, carrot, celery and chilli to the dish and cook, stirring, for 5 minutes until soft. Stir in the pancetta and cook for 5 minutes until golden. Add the garlic, tomato, ham hock, bay leaves, thyme and broth and bring to the boil.

4 Cover the dish with the lid and place in the oven to cook for 2 hours until the meat is falling off the bone.

5 Add the parsnip, sweet potato, swede, sausages and duck legs to the dish.

6 Return the dish, uncovered, to the oven and cook for 30 minutes until the sausages are cooked through.

7 Remove the ham hock from the cassoulet and, when it is cool enough to handle, discard the skin and bone and shred the meat. Add the meat to the cassoulet, season with salt and pepper and sprinkle over the parsley.

PRESSURE COOKER Using your pressure cooker over medium–high heat, follow steps **2**–**3**, but add only 700 ml of broth rather than 1 litre. Close the lid and lock it, then bring the cooker to high pressure and cook over medium heat for 20 minutes. Naturally release the pressure before opening the lid. Follow step **5**, close and lock the lid, then bring the cooker to high pressure and cook over medium heat for 5 minutes. Let the pressure drop naturally before opening the lid. Follow step **7**.

SLOW COOKER Follow steps **1**–**4**, but add only 700 ml of broth rather than 1 litre. Transfer all the ingredients from the casserole dish to your slow cooker. Follow step **5**, cover with the lid and cook on low for 8½ hours. Follow step **7**.

The pressure is on, as the butter chicken recipe that featured in my book *Family Food* was voted the most popular family dish amongst readers. So, now, the question is: can I top it? I think this chicken tikka masala will give the butter chicken a run for its money in the flavour stakes and will become a favourite once you give it a try. Coconut yoghurt is used here, which gives a wonderful sweetness. If you are looking for a little more heat, add extra cayenne pepper.

SERVES 4

Chicken TIKKA MASALA

220 g coconut yoghurt (for a recipe, see page 235)

1½ teaspoons sea salt

800 g chicken thigh fillets, cut into 2 cm pieces

3 tablespoons coconut oil

1½ onions, chopped

½ red capsicum, diced

1 teaspoon finely chopped coriander stalks

8 green cardamom pods, bruised

1 cinnamon stick

1½ teaspoons paprika

4 tablespoons tomato paste

1–2 pinches of cayenne pepper

4 tomatoes (about 400 g), chopped

250 ml (1 cup) Chicken Bone Broth (page 234)

150 ml coconut cream

1½ teaspoons lemon juice

Garlic spice mixture

2 garlic cloves, finely grated

1 tablespoon finely grated ginger

½ teaspoon ground turmeric

2½ teaspoons garam masala

2 teaspoons ground coriander

2 teaspoons ground cumin

To serve

Cauliflower Rice (page 233)

coriander leaves

❶ To make the garlic spice mixture, combine all the ingredients in a bowl.

❷ Place 1 tablespoon of the garlic spice mixture, the coconut yoghurt and salt in a non-reactive bowl and mix to combine. Add the chicken, toss to evenly coat, cover with plastic wrap and marinate in the fridge for 2 hours.

❸ Melt 1 tablespoon of the oil in a wok or large frying pan over medium–high heat. Add the chicken in batches and seal for 2 minutes on each side until golden and just starting to char, then remove from the pan.

❹ Wipe the pan clean, add the remaining oil and the onion and cook over medium heat for 5 minutes until the onion is soft. Add the capsicum and coriander stalk and cook for a further 5 minutes to soften.

❺ Stir in the remaining garlic spice mixture, the cardamom, cinnamon stick and paprika and cook for 30 seconds until fragrant. Add the tomato paste and cayenne pepper and cook for 1 minute. Add the tomato and cook for 5 minutes, stirring constantly, until broken down. Pour in the broth and coconut cream, bring to the boil and add the chicken.

❻ Reduce the heat to low and simmer for 30 minutes until the chicken is cooked through and the sauce has thickened.

❼ Stir through the lemon juice and season with salt if needed. Serve with the cauliflower rice and a sprinkle of coriander leaves.

PRESSURE COOKER Follow steps ❶–❷. Using your pressure cooker over medium–high heat, follow steps ❸–❺. Close the lid and lock it, then bring the cooker to high pressure and cook over medium heat for 6 minutes. Let the pressure drop naturally before opening the lid. Follow step ❼.

SLOW COOKER Follow steps ❶–❺, then transfer the chicken and all the ingredients in the wok or pan to your slow cooker. Cover and cook on high for 4 hours, or on low for 8 hours. Follow step ❼.

I was fortunate enough to work with the amazing Australian journalist Indira Naidoo a few years ago and she prepared her family's South African curry for me. I was blown away by the flavour. The thing about curries is, yes, there are lots of ingredients, but if you stock your pantry well, you can create dishes like this anytime. Thanks, Indira, for this wonderful recipe and for filling countless kitchens with awesome aromas.

SOUTH AFRICAN
SERVES 4–6 *Chicken Curry*

3 tablespoons coconut oil or
   good-quality animal fat*
8 chicken drumsticks
2 onions, sliced
5 garlic cloves, chopped
2 tablespoons finely grated ginger
2 cinnamon sticks
5 green cardamom pods, bruised
4 whole cloves
2 bay leaves
10 fresh curry leaves
1½ teaspoons ground fennel
1½ teaspoons ground coriander
1½ teaspoons ground turmeric
1 teaspoon smoked paprika
1 teaspoon mild curry powder
2 teaspoons sea salt
3 large tomatoes, chopped
1 large zucchini, sliced
400 ml Chicken Bone Broth
   (page 234) or water

* See Glossary

❶ Preheat the oven to 180°C.

❷ Melt 2 tablespoons of the oil or fat in a large flameproof casserole dish over medium heat. Add the chicken and cook on all sides for 2 minutes until golden, then remove from the dish.

❸ Melt the remaining oil or fat in the dish, add the onion and cook for 5–8 minutes until starting to caramelise. Add the garlic and ginger and cook, stirring frequently, for 1 minute until softened. Stir in the cinnamon, cardamom, cloves, bay leaves and curry leaves and fry for 1 minute until fragrant. Reduce the heat to medium–low, add the ground spices and salt and fry, stirring occasionally, for 1 minute until fragrant.

❹ Increase the heat to medium, add the chicken, tomato, zucchini and broth or water and bring to the boil.

❺ Transfer the dish to the oven and bake, basting and turning the chicken from time to time, for 40 minutes until the chicken is cooked through.

PRESSURE COOKER Follow steps ❷–❸, using your pressure cooker, then add the chicken, tomatoes, zucchini and 280 ml of broth or water. Close the lid and lock it, then bring the cooker to high pressure over high heat. Reduce the heat to medium and cook for 10 minutes. Let the pressure drop naturally before opening the lid.

SLOW COOKER Follow steps ❷–❸. Transfer the spiced onion mixture, the chicken, tomato, zucchini and 280 ml of broth or water to your slow cooker. Cover and cook on low for 6 hours until the chicken is cooked through.

Recently, I cooked up some leftover confit duck for breakfast with some greens and cabbage. It was the best culinary start to my day ever! I decided then and there that I would never again eat a boring dish for breakfast. Now my brekkies feature curries, roasts, braises, soups or any leftovers from the night before. Sounds crazy? I dare you to try it and see how crazy it really is. You'll need to begin this recipe 2 days ahead.

SERVES 4

Crispy DUCK CONFIT

4 tablespoons fine sea salt

1 tablespoon juniper berries

1 teaspoon finely grated orange zest

2 tablespoons orange juice

4 duck legs

5 thyme sprigs

4 bay leaves

4 garlic cloves

800 g duck or goose fat, coconut oil or good-quality animal fat*, melted (see tip)

See Glossary

❶ Combine the salt, juniper berries and orange zest and juice in a large shallow bowl and mix well. Rub the salt mixture into the duck to evenly coat. Cover with plastic wrap and refrigerate for 12 hours or, for best results, 24 hours.

❷ Preheat the oven to 100°C.

❸ Rinse the duck legs, then pat dry with paper towel. Place the duck legs in a single layer in a casserole dish. Add the thyme, bay leaves and garlic and pour on the fat or oil to completely submerge the duck legs.

❹ Bake the duck legs in the oven for 2 hours until very tender.

❺ Allow the duck confit to cool completely at room temperature, then refrigerate overnight.

❻ When ready to crisp the duck legs, preheat the oven to 220°C. Remove the duck legs from the fat or oil and pat dry with paper towel, being careful not to break the skin. Reserve the fat or oil for another use.

❼ Arrange the duck legs in a single layer in a lightly greased roasting tin and bake in the oven for 20–25 minutes until golden. Sprinkle with a little salt if needed and serve with your favourite salad or side.

SLOW COOKER Follow step ❶, then follow step ❸, using your slow cooker. Cover with the lid and cook on low for 6–8 hours until the duck is tender and falling away from the bone. Follow steps ❺–❼.

Tip I often use half duck fat and half coconut oil for making confit dishes at home, and it produces a great result.

There is something very comforting about slowly cooking a whole chook in an aromatic broth and plating it up for the family. Here, for extra flavour, I have added a delicious chicken liver stuffing. You can, of course, leave out the stuffing if you wish, but any chance of getting liver – the most nutrient-dense ingredient on earth – into a dish is a good idea to me.

Braised CHICKEN with

SERVES 4–6 PISTACHIO AND LIVER STUFFING

1 × 1.8 kg chicken
4 garlic cloves, sliced
1 onion, sliced
6 Dutch carrots, leafy tops trimmed
6 thyme sprigs
2 bay leaves
1 large swede, cut into 3 cm pieces
1 celery stalk, cut into 3 cm pieces
1 leek, white part only, cut on an
    angle into 2 cm thick pieces
800 ml Chicken Bone Broth
    (page 234)
1 tablespoon apple cider vinegar
100 ml dry white wine
¼ teaspoon celery seeds
1 tablespoon finely chopped flat-leaf
    parsley leaves
sea salt and freshly ground
    black pepper

Stuffing
60 g pistachio nuts (activated if
    possible*), toasted and chopped
3 garlic cloves, finely chopped
3 tablespoons finely chopped flat-
    leaf parsley leaves
5 chicken livers, trimmed and finely
    chopped
2 slices of rindless bacon, chopped
4 tablespoons LSA* or flaxseed meal
2 eggs, beaten
1 tablespoon coconut oil

* See Glossary

❶ Preheat the oven to 160°C.

❷ To make the stuffing, combine all the ingredients in a bowl and mix well.

❸ Fill the chicken cavity with the stuffing and tie the legs together with kitchen string. Place the chicken in a large flameproof casserole dish.

❹ Arrange the garlic, onion, carrots, thyme, bay leaves, swede, celery and leek around the chicken. Pour in the broth, vinegar and wine, sprinkle over the celery seeds and half the parsley and season with salt and pepper.

❺ Cover the dish with a tight-fitting lid or a double layer of foil and transfer to the oven to cook for 3 hours until the chicken is cooked through.

❻ Place the chicken on a chopping board and cover with foil to keep warm. Remove all the vegetables from the dish with a slotted spoon.

❼ Place the dish on the stovetop, bring to the boil and cook for about 15 minutes until the braising liquid is reduced by one-third. Mix in the remaining parsley and season with salt and pepper if needed.

❽ Transfer the chicken and reduced braising liquid to a platter, remove the string and serve with the vegetables.

PRESSURE COOKER Follow step ❷. Using your pressure cooker, follow steps ❸–❹. Close and lock the lid, then bring the cooker to high pressure and cook over medium heat for 35 minutes. Let the pressure drop naturally before opening the lid. Follow steps ❻–❽.

SLOW COOKER Follow steps ❷–❹, using your slow cooker. Cover and cook on low for 8–10 hours until the chicken is cooked through. Follow step ❼, reducing the braising liquid in a saucepan, then follow step ❽.

I was never a fan of olives as a kid and I can't help but think about what I missed out on. This is why I encourage my daughters to try new food. If they don't like it, they can try it again, and one day they may finally get a taste for it. This dish is a wonderful way to introduce some new ingredients to your kids. You could swap out the drumsticks and use marylands or thighs (with the skin on), or a whole chicken.

Roast DRUMSTICKS
SERVES 4 **WITH OLIVES AND CAPERS**

8 chicken drumsticks

sea salt and freshly ground
    black pepper

3 tablespoons apple cider vinegar

3 tablespoons coconut oil or
    good-quality animal fat*

1 teaspoon fennel seeds, crushed

4 garlic cloves, finely chopped

120 g pitted green olives

3 tablespoons salted baby capers,
    rinsed and patted dry

4 bay leaves

200 ml Chicken Bone Broth
    (page 234)

100 ml dry white wine

½ teaspoon paprika

1 large handful of oregano leaves

* See Glossary

❶ Season the drumsticks with salt and pepper, place in a large bowl and set aside.

❷ In another bowl, combine the vinegar, oil or fat, fennel seeds and garlic and mix well. Pour over the chicken and rub into the skin. Cover with plastic wrap and place in the fridge for 1 hour to marinate.

❸ Preheat the oven to 200°C.

❹ Transfer the chicken to a roasting tin and pour over the marinade. Scatter on the olives, capers and bay leaves, pour on the broth and wine and sprinkle the paprika over the chicken.

❺ Place the chicken in the oven and roast, occasionally basting with the juices in the tin, for 40 minutes until the drumsticks are cooked through and golden. Season with salt and pepper if needed, scatter over the oregano and serve with your choice of sides.

Whether you're a home cook or a top chef, when it comes to putting a dish on the table, it's all about flavour. These days I am less concerned about appearances and the latest ingredients and techniques and am more focused on how to incorporate layers of deliciousness into the food I serve at my restaurants and at home. Here is a wonderful example of a dish that has so many layers of flavour it will become a firm family favourite.

SERVES 4

Pepper CHICKEN MASALA

800 g chicken thigh fillets

sea salt and freshly ground
    black pepper

3 tablespoons coconut oil or
    good-quality animal fat*

1 teaspoon brown mustard seeds

2 onions, chopped

1 tablespoon tomato paste

4 garlic cloves, chopped

2½ teaspoons finely grated ginger

10 fresh curry leaves

1 × 400 g can diced tomatoes
    (or 400 g tomatoes, diced)

250 ml (1 cup) Chicken Bone Broth
    (page 234)

Zucchini, Cauliflower or Broccoli
    Rice (pages 245, 233 and 232),
    to serve

Spice mix

2 teaspoons cumin seeds

3 teaspoons coriander seeds

½ teaspoon fennel seeds

½ teaspoon chilli flakes

2 teaspoons black peppercorns

1 cinnamon stick

3 green cardamom pods, bruised

½ teaspoon ground turmeric

* See Glossary

❶ To make the spice mix, toast all the spices except the turmeric in a large frying pan over medium heat for 1 minute until fragrant. Remove from the pan, allow to cool, then grind to a coarse powder using a mortar and pestle or a spice grinder. Mix in the turmeric.

❷ Coat the chicken with the spice mix, season with salt and set aside.

❸ Melt the oil or fat in the pan over medium heat. Add the mustard seeds and cook for 10 seconds until they start to pop. Add the onion and cook for 5 minutes until the onion is soft and starting to colour. Stir in the tomato paste, garlic, ginger and curry leaves and cook, stirring occasionally, for 1 minute until fragrant.

❹ Add the spiced chicken to the pan and cook, turning occasionally, for 5 minutes until lightly golden.

❺ Stir through the tomatoes and broth and bring to the boil.

❻ Reduce the heat to low and simmer for 20 minutes until the chicken is cooked and the sauce is thick.

❼ Season with salt and pepper if needed. Serve with your choice of veggie rice.

PRESSURE COOKER Follow steps ❶–❷. Using your pressure cooker over medium heat, follow steps ❸–❹. Follow step ❺, but add only 180 ml of broth rather than 250 ml. Close the lid and lock it, then bring the cooker to high pressure and cook over medium heat for 10 minutes. Let the pressure drop naturally before opening the lid. Follow step ❼.

SLOW COOKER Follow steps ❶–❹, then transfer the browned chicken and the ingredients from the pan to your slow cooker. Follow step ❺, but add only 180 ml of broth rather than 250 ml. Cover and cook on high for 2 hours. Follow step ❼.

Roast chicken is one of our favourite family dishes and every time we cook it we play around with different flavours. You can go Italian with rosemary, garlic and lemon, then next time take a trip to India with a spicy curry seasoning, or try Argentinean with some chimichurri. I think you get where this can lead to – a lifetime of experimenting. This recipe is inspired by the amazing Ethiopian spice blend berbere.

Ethiopian BERBERE Roast Chicken

SERVES 4–6

1 × 1.8 kg chicken
2 tablespoons coconut oil or
    good-quality animal fat*
sea salt and freshly ground
    black pepper
1 lemon, cut into wedges
6 silverbeet leaves, chopped into
    large pieces
2 tablespoons olive oil

Spice mix
3 tablespoons paprika
2 teaspoons garlic powder
1 teaspoon ground ginger
1 teaspoon ground cumin
1 teaspoon onion powder
1 teaspoon freshly ground
    black pepper
½ teaspoon ground fenugreek
2 teaspoons ground turmeric
½ teaspoon sea salt
½ teaspoon ground cardamom
¼ teaspoon ground cloves

See Glossary

❶ Preheat the oven to 180°C.

❷ Combine the spice mix ingredients in a bowl and mix well.

❸ Place the chicken in a roasting tin. Rub the oil or fat into the chicken, then coat evenly with 3½ tablespoons of the spice mix and season with salt and pepper. Tie the legs together with kitchen string. Arrange the lemon wedges around the chicken and roast in the oven for 30 minutes, basting with the oil in the tin from time to time, until lightly golden.

❹ Remove the lemon from the tin and set aside. Pour in 125 ml of water, cover with foil and return to the oven to roast for a further 40 minutes until the chicken is cooked through. Transfer the chicken to a plate, cover with foil and keep warm.

❺ Add the silverbeet to the tin and pour in 500 ml of boiling water, then tightly cover with foil and cook in the oven for a further 10 minutes until wilted. Strain and discard the water, season the silverbeet with salt and pepper and drizzle over the olive oil.

❻ Cut the chicken into pieces and serve with the wilted silverbeet and roasted lemon wedges to squeeze over the chicken.

Tip Leftover spice mix can be stored in a glass jar in the pantry for up to 3 months.

I think curries are one of the best things in the world to cook and eat. At home we play around with a different one every week. This is a very simple but impressive dish that is all about harmony and balance. I love the aromatic flavours that permeate our kitchen and the anticipation of waiting to enjoy the meltingly tender meat enveloped in a luscious, tantalising sauce. If you are not a fan of spice, halve the amount of chilli or leave it out altogether.

SERVES 6

Duck Leg CURRY

6 duck legs (about 1.2 kg)

2 tablespoons duck fat or coconut oil

sea salt and freshly ground
    black pepper

1 onion, finely chopped

10 fresh curry leaves

4 tablespoons curry powder

750 ml (3 cups) Beef or Chicken
    Bone Broth (pages 230 and 234)

1 × 400 g can diced tomatoes
    (or 400 g tomatoes, diced)

6 French shallots, halved

Curry paste

6 cm piece of ginger, chopped

6 garlic cloves, peeled

2.5 cm piece of fresh turmeric,
    chopped (or 1 teaspoon ground
    turmeric)

1–2 long red chillies, deseeded and
    chopped (leave half the seeds
    in if you like it spicy)

❶ To make the curry paste, place the ginger, garlic, turmeric, chilli and 3 tablespoons of water in the bowl of a food processor and whiz to a fine paste.

❷ Coat the duck legs with 1 tablespoon of the fat and season with salt and pepper. Heat a large frying pan over medium–high heat. Add the duck legs in batches and brown on all sides for 2 minutes until golden, then remove from the pan.

❸ Reduce the heat to medium, add the remaining fat and the onion and sauté for 5 minutes until translucent. Stir in the curry paste and curry leaves and cook for 1 minute, then add the curry powder and sauté for 30 seconds until fragrant. Pour in the broth and tomatoes, add the shallot and duck legs and season.

❹ Bring the curry to the boil, then reduce the heat to low. Cover with a lid and simmer for 2 hours until the meat is falling off the bone.

❺ Remove the duck legs from the curry and set aside, covered in foil to keep warm.

❻ Skim the layer of fat from the top of the curry (and reserve for other dishes). Bring the curry to the boil and cook until reduced to a thick sauce consistency, about 10 minutes. Return the duck legs to the curry and serve.

PRESSURE COOKER Follow step ❶. Using your pressure cooker over medium–high heat, follow steps ❷–❸, but add only 500 ml broth rather than 750 ml. Close the lid and lock it, then bring the cooker to high pressure and cook over medium heat for 50 minutes. Let the pressure drop naturally before opening the lid. Follow steps ❺–❻.

SLOW COOKER Follow steps ❶–❸, but add only 500 ml broth rather than 750 ml. Transfer all the ingredients from the pan to your slow cooker. Cover with the lid and cook on low for 8 hours. Follow steps ❺–❻, using a saucepan to reduce the sauce.

I have jazzed up this family classic and created a Korean-style chicken meatloaf. Meatloaf also works wonderfully when you make individual portions in muffin tins. If you want to add a little more nutritional goodness, try adding some minced chicken livers to the mix.

Korean Chicken MEATLOAF
SERVES 6 WITH KIMCHI AND SSAMJANG GLAZE

2 spring onions, finely sliced
1 tablespoon sesame seeds, toasted

Meatloaf
600 g chicken mince
400 g pork mince
160 g kimchi (for a recipe, see page 238), plus extra to serve
2 tablespoons coconut oil
1 red onion, finely chopped
1 tablespoon finely grated ginger
3 garlic cloves, finely chopped
50 g (scant ½ cup) almond meal
2 tablespoons finely chopped coriander leaves
1 egg
1 tablespoon tamari or coconut aminos*
2 teaspoons sesame oil
1 teaspoon sea salt
¼ teaspoon freshly ground black pepper

Ssamjang glaze
1 tablespoon sriracha or Fermented Hot Chilli Sauce (page 236)
1 tablespoon apple cider vinegar
2 tablespoons honey
1½ teaspoons finely grated ginger
1 tablespoon tomato paste

* See Glossary

❶ Preheat the oven to 180ºC. Line the base and sides of a 12 cm × 20 cm loaf tin with a piece of baking paper, cutting into the corners to fit and allowing the paper to extend 5 cm above the sides.

❷ Place all the meatloaf ingredients in a bowl and mix until well combined. Firmly pack the meat mixture into the prepared tin, then bake in the oven for 25 minutes.

❸ Meanwhile, to make the ssamjang glaze, combine all the ingredients in a bowl and mix well.

❹ Remove the meatloaf from the oven and baste the top with half the glaze. Return to the oven and bake for 20 minutes until cooked through. To test if the meatloaf is cooked, insert a thermometer into the centre; if it reaches at least 70ºC, it's ready.

❺ Allow the meatloaf to rest in a warm place for 10 minutes before turning out of the tin. Spoon over the remaining glaze, then sprinkle on some kimchi, spring onion and sesame seeds. Slice and serve with your favourite salad or roasted vegetables.

If you have never tried making a tagine, I urge you to give this a go. I have used a whole chicken because I like the look of an entire roast bird on the dinner table; however, to speed up the process, swap out the whole chook for smaller cuts (but steer clear of breast fillets as they have a tendency to dry out). Using chermoula to marinate the chicken and to flavour the sauce is brilliant.

Whole Chicken TAGINE

Chermoula (page 233)

1 × 1.8 kg chicken

2 tablespoons coconut oil

2 onions, sliced

1 teaspoon finely grated ginger

500 g kent pumpkin, cut into thick wedges

2 pinches of saffron threads

300 ml hot Chicken Bone Broth (page 234)

4 large preserved lemon quarters, flesh removed, rind sliced

8 medjool dates, pitted

20 pitted black or green olives

❶ Spoon the chermoula over the chicken to coat evenly. Place the chicken in a container, cover and transfer to the fridge to marinate for 4 hours or overnight.

❷ Preheat the oven to 180°C.

❸ Melt the oil in a tagine or flameproof casserole dish over medium–low heat. Add the onion and ginger and cook for 4–5 minutes until soft but not coloured.

❹ Place the marinated chicken on top of the onion mixture and pour in the marinade. Arrange the pumpkin wedges around the chicken. Stir the saffron into the hot broth and pour over the chicken, then scatter on the preserved lemon, dates and olives.

❺ Transfer the dish to the oven and cook for 20 minutes until the chicken is lightly golden. Cover with the lid and cook, basting the chicken occasionally with the juices in the dish, for 45–60 minutes until the chicken is cooked through and the juices run clear. Serve with your favourite side.

PRESSURE COOKER Follow step ❶. Using your pressure cooker over medium heat, follow step ❸. Follow step ❹, but add only 250 ml of broth rather than 300 ml. Close the lid and lock it, then bring the cooker to high pressure over medium–low heat and cook for 35 minutes. Let the pressure drop naturally before opening the lid. You can serve the chicken as is, or if you would like some colour on it, transfer the chicken to a roasting tin and cook in a 200°C oven for 20–30 minutes until golden.

SLOW COOKER Follow step ❶. Follow step ❸, using a small frying pan, then transfer the ingredients from the frying pan to your slow cooker. Follow step ❹, but add only 210 ml of broth rather than 300 ml. Cover and cook on low for 6–8 hours until the chicken is cooked through. You can serve the chicken as is, or if you would like some colour on it, remove the dish from the slow cooker and place it in a 200°C oven for 20–30 minutes until the chicken is golden.

I know I am breaking with tradition here by making chicken instead of lamb rogan josh, but if you think about it, all the classic dishes in the world have somehow been reworked in their own special way. Rogan josh is a dish of Persian origin that became a staple in Kashmiri cuisine and is now very popular in British curry houses. I am sure it has many variations from kitchen to kitchen. Here is a version that is sure to sing at your next dinner party.

SERVES 4–6

ROGAN JOSH *Chicken*

4 tablespoons coconut oil

2 onions, chopped

5 garlic cloves, chopped

1½ tablespoons finely grated ginger

½ teaspoon ground cloves

1½ teaspoons ground turmeric

1 teaspoon ground cardamom

1 teaspoon fennel seeds

2 teaspoons ground coriander

2 teaspoons ground cumin

2 teaspoons paprika

½ teaspoon chilli powder

2 cinnamon sticks

2 bay leaves

1 × 400 g can whole peeled tomatoes, crushed (or 400 g tomatoes, diced)

3 tablespoons Chicken Bone Broth (page 234)

sea salt and freshly ground black pepper

1 kg chicken thigh fillets, cut into 2 cm pieces

juice of ½ lemon

To serve

coriander leaves

Cauliflower Rice (page 233)

Raita (page 39)

1 long green chilli, finely sliced

❶ Heat the coconut oil in a large saucepan over medium heat. Add the onion and sauté for 5 minutes until translucent. Reduce the heat to low and stir in the garlic, ginger, spices and bay leaves and cook, stirring frequently, for 3 minutes. Add the tomatoes and cook for 1 minute, then pour in the broth and mix well. Season with salt and pepper.

❷ Increase the heat to medium and bring the sauce to a simmer. Add the chicken and stir until well coated with the sauce.

❸ Cover the pan with a lid, reduce the heat to low and cook, stirring occasionally, for 20–25 minutes until the chicken is cooked through and the sauce has thickened.

❹ Stir the lemon juice into the curry, scatter on the coriander leaves and serve with the cauliflower rice, raita and chilli.

PRESSURE COOKER Using your pressure cooker over medium–high heat, follow steps ❶–❷. Close the lid and lock it, then bring the cooker to high pressure and cook over medium heat for 10 minutes. Let the pressure drop naturally before opening the lid. Follow step ❹.

SLOW COOKER Follow steps ❶–❷, then transfer all the ingredients from the saucepan to your slow cooker. Cover with the lid and cook on low for 4–6 hours. Follow step ❹.

Renowned author and paleo advocate Danielle Walker from *Against All Grain* taught me this simple and delicious midweek family dinner. I visited Danielle to interview her and cook with her for my TV series. She was such a delight to work with. I loved her approach to cooking and I am sure you will, too. Thanks, Danielle, for the recipe, and keep inspiring millions of people.

SERVES 4

PAD SEE EW

5 carrots (about 500 g in total)

2 tablespoons coconut oil

6 garlic cloves, finely chopped

600 g chicken breast or thigh fillets, thinly sliced on the diagonal

450 g broccolini, chopped into 5 cm lengths

4 tablespoons tamari or coconut aminos*

2 eggs

To serve

Thai basil leaves

sliced spring onion

black and white sesame seeds

lime wedges

* *See Glossary*

❶ To make the carrot noodles, use the wide ribbon blade on a vegetable spiraliser. Alternatively, place the carrots on a chopping board and, using a vegetable peeler, peel into thin, wide ribbons. (Save the leftover trimmings for broths or soups.)

❷ Melt the oil in a wok or deep frying pan over medium heat. Add the garlic and chicken and stir-fry for 2 minutes until the chicken changes colour.

❸ Add the broccolini and tamari or coconut aminos to the pan and cook for 5 minutes until the broccolini is softened. Add the carrot noodles and stir-fry for another 3 minutes.

❹ Push the stir-fry aside in the pan. Crack in the eggs, stir vigorously to scramble them and cook for 2 minutes until set. Mix everything together and serve immediately with the basil leaves, spring onion and sesame seeds scattered over the top and the lime wedges on the side.

This French classic – chicken in wine – is a wonderful dish to cook on cooler nights when you have a great bottle of red that you want to put to good use. If you are avoiding alcohol, simply omit the wine and use more chicken stock. Here, I have thickened the sauce with tapioca flour. Some people find it bloating, so you may like to leave it out or use coconut flour or ground almonds in its place. You will need to begin this recipe 2 days ahead.

SERVES 6

COQ AU VIN

6 chicken marylands, drumstick
    and thigh separated
3 tablespoons coconut oil or
    good-quality animal fat*
150 g rindless bacon, finely chopped
900 ml Chicken Bone Broth
    (page 234)
200 g button mushrooms, halved
sea salt
2 tablespoons tapioca flour*
1 handful of flat-leaf parsley leaves,
    to serve

Marinade
600 ml preservative-free red wine
2 bay leaves
2 rosemary sprigs
4 thyme sprigs
1 onion, finely chopped
1 carrot, finely chopped
1 celery stalk, finely chopped
3 garlic cloves, finely chopped
½ teaspoon freshly ground
    black pepper

* See Glossary

❶ Combine the marinade ingredients in a large non-reactive dish. Add the chicken and submerge in the marinade, cover and place in the fridge overnight.

❷ Preheat the oven to 160°C.

❸ Remove the chicken from the marinade. Strain the marinade, reserving the liquid and vegetables separately. Pat the chicken dry with paper towel.

❹ Melt the oil or fat in a large flameproof casserole dish over medium–high heat. Add the chicken in batches and cook on all sides for 2 minutes until golden brown, then remove from the dish and set aside.

❺ Add the reserved vegetables and the bacon to the dish and cook, stirring occasionally, for 8 minutes until golden. Pour in the reserved marinade, bring to the boil and cook until reduced by half, about 4 minutes.

❻ Pour in the broth, then add the chicken and mushrooms and season with salt.

❼ Cover tightly and bake for 1 hour and 20 minutes until the chicken is tender.

❽ Remove the chicken, place in a serving dish, cover and keep warm. Simmer the broth over medium–high heat for 10 minutes until reduced by more than half.

❾ Mix 3 tablespoons of cold water with the tapioca flour, then stir into the reduced broth and simmer for 2 minutes to thicken. Pour over the chicken, then sprinkle on the parsley leaves. Serve with mashed parsnip or cauliflower.

PRESSURE COOKER Follow steps ❶ and ❸. Using your pressure cooker over medium–high heat, follow steps ❹–❻, but add only 630 ml of broth rather than 900 ml. Close the lid and lock it, then bring the cooker to high pressure and cook over medium heat for 30 minutes. Let the pressure drop naturally before opening the lid. Follow steps ❽–❾.

SLOW COOKER Follow steps ❶ and ❸–❺. Transfer the ingredients from the casserole dish to your slow cooker. Follow step ❻, but add only 630 ml of broth rather than 900 ml. Cover and cook on low for 8 hours. Follow step ❽, using a saucepan. Follow step ❾.

I love how simple and flavoursome chicken is, and the fact that we can buy free-range organic chicken in most supermarkets needs to be celebrated in family-friendly dishes such as this. As it is sweetened with pomegranate molasses and honey, which shouldn't be over-consumed, consider this recipe as a bit of a treat. Serve with some green veg on the side.

Middle Eastern CHICKEN

SERVES 4–6 WITH SPICED RICE

10 chicken drumsticks
sea salt and freshly ground
    black pepper

Middle Eastern marinade
4 tablespoons pomegranate
    molasses*
1 tablespoon honey
2 tablespoons coconut oil or
    good-quality animal fat*, melted
2 garlic cloves, finely chopped
2 tablespoons apple cider vinegar
2 tablespoons Turkish Spice Blend
    (page 244)
½ teaspoon ground cumin

To serve
1–2 pinches of sumac*
seeds from ½ pomegranate
1 handful of mint leaves
Spiced Rice (page 241)

* See Glossary

① To make the marinade, place all the ingredients in a large bowl and whisk to combine.

② Add the chicken to the marinade and mix to evenly coat. Season with salt and pepper, cover and marinate in the fridge for 1 hour or, for best results, overnight.

③ Preheat the oven to 200ºC.

④ Transfer the chicken and the marinade to a large roasting tin, spreading the drumsticks out in a single layer. Roast in the oven, basting the chicken a few times with the marinade, for 30–35 minutes until the chicken is cooked through and the skin is golden.

⑤ Arrange the chicken on a large platter, sprinkle over the sumac, pomegranate seeds and mint leaves and serve with the spiced rice.

As you can probably tell by now, I absolutely adore curries in all guises: from sour curries flavoured with tamarind to sweeter curries enhanced with fruit and pungent curries laced with shrimp paste and fish sauce. This tried-and-tested favourite features a wonderful array of medicinal spices and, to round it all out and add an element of acidity and sweetness, is finished with cherry tomatoes.

CHICKEN CURRY

SERVES 4–6 *with Heirloom Tomatoes*

2 tablespoons coriander seeds

3 green cardamom pods, bruised

1 teaspoon ground turmeric

2½ teaspoons cumin seeds

2 teaspoons paprika

3 long red chillies, deseeded and chopped

5 red Asian shallots, finely sliced

5 cm piece of ginger, finely sliced

4 garlic cloves, finely chopped

1 teaspoon sea salt

2 tablespoons tomato paste

1.4 kg chicken pieces (thighs, drumsticks, wings), bone in

3 tablespoons coconut oil or good-quality animal fat*

435 ml (1¾ cups) Chicken Bone Broth (page 234)

1 cinnamon stick, broken

250 g heirloom cherry tomatoes

freshly ground black pepper

coriander leaves, to serve

* See Glossary

❶ Combine the coriander seeds, cardamom, turmeric and cumin seeds in a large, deep frying pan over medium heat and toast, tossing occasionally, for 1 minute until fragrant. Remove from the pan. Finely grind the toasted spices using a spice grinder or a mortar and pestle. Transfer to a small bowl and stir through the paprika.

❷ Place the chilli, shallot, ginger, garlic, salt, tomato paste, ground spices and 4 tablespoons of water in the bowl of a food processor and process to a fine paste.

❸ Put the chicken pieces in a large bowl, add the spice paste and toss to coat well. Cover with plastic wrap and marinate in the fridge for 2 hours or, for best results, overnight.

❹ Melt the oil or fat in the pan over medium heat. Add the chicken and marinade and fry for 5 minutes until the chicken is brown all over.

❺ Add the broth and cinnamon to the pan and simmer, covered, for 35 minutes.

❻ Add the tomatoes to the curry and cook for 5 minutes until the chicken is cooked through.

❼ Season with salt and pepper if needed. Arrange the chicken on a large platter, pour on the sauce and scatter over the coriander leaves.

PRESSURE COOKER Follow steps ❶–❸. Using your pressure cooker over medium heat, follow step ❹. Add the cinnamon and 350 ml of broth. Close the lid and lock it, then bring the cooker to high pressure and cook over medium heat for 15 minutes. Let the pressure drop naturally before opening the lid. Reduce the heat to medium, add the tomatoes and cook, uncovered, for 5 minutes. Follow step ❼.

SLOW COOKER Follow steps ❶–❹, then transfer the browned chicken to your slow cooker. Add the cinnamon and 300 ml of broth. Cover and cook on low for 6 hours. Set to medium, add the tomatoes, cover and cook for 15 minutes. Follow step ❼.

This South American–inspired dish is one of my favourites and the kids love it, too. The addition of paprika, cumin, honey, garlic and chilli elevates the classic roast chicken to another level. Any leftover coriander sauce is great tossed through a salad of roasted sweet potato and broccoli.

Peruvian-style
ROAST CHICKEN
SERVES 6 **WITH CORIANDER SAUCE**

3 tablespoons coconut oil or
   good-quality animal fat*, melted
3 garlic cloves, finely chopped
3 teaspoons paprika
1 tablespoon ground cumin
1 tablespoon honey
juice of 2 limes
1½ teaspoons sea salt
1 teaspoon freshly ground
   black pepper
1 × 1.8 kg chicken
2 garlic bulbs, cut in half
   horizontally
4 French shallots, cut into wedges
4 jalapeno chillies, cut in half
   lengthways
250 ml (1 cup) Chicken Bone Broth
   (page 234) or water

Coriander sauce
1 jalapeno chilli, deseeded and
   roughly chopped (leave half the
   seeds in if you like it spicy)
1 large handful of coriander leaves,
   roughly chopped
3 garlic cloves, chopped
150 g mayonnaise (for a recipe, see
   page 239)
1 tablespoon lime juice
2 tablespoons extra-virgin olive oil
sea salt and freshly ground
   black pepper

❶ Combine the oil or fat, chopped garlic, paprika, cumin, honey, lime juice, salt and pepper in a large bowl and mix well. Add the chicken and rub in the marinade to evenly coat. Cover and marinate in the fridge for at least 6 hours or, for best results, overnight.

❷ Preheat the oven to 200ºC.

❸ Transfer the chicken and any marinade in the bowl to a large casserole dish. Tie the legs together with kitchen string. Scatter the garlic bulbs, shallot and chilli around the chicken, then pour in the broth. Place in the oven and roast, basting occasionally with the juices in the dish, for 30 minutes until the chicken is golden. Reduce the temperature to 180ºC, cover with foil and continue to cook, basting occasionally, for 45 minutes until the chicken is cooked through. Allow the chicken to rest, covered with foil, for 15 minutes.

❹ Meanwhile, to make the coriander sauce, combine all the ingredients in the bowl of a food processor and whiz until smooth. Season with salt and pepper.

❺ Carve the chicken and serve with the coriander sauce and roasted vegetables.

This dish should be enjoyed with friends and family. It is full of warming spices and I love to serve it with a refreshing Asian cucumber salad or coleslaw, some pan-tossed spiced okra and fermented veg on the side.

SERVES 4–6

Malaysian ROAST CHICKEN

2½ tablespoons coriander seeds

½ cinnamon stick

3 green cardamom pods, bruised

4 whole cloves

½ teaspoon ground turmeric

2 teaspoons cumin seeds

4 dried long red chillies, soaked in warm water for 10 minutes

4 red Asian shallots, finely sliced

3 cm piece of ginger, chopped

1 lemongrass stalk, white part only, chopped

1 teaspoon sea salt

4 garlic cloves, finely chopped

2 tablespoons honey or coconut sugar

4 tablespoons apple cider vinegar

2 tablespoons coconut oil or good-quality animal fat*

1.4 kg chicken marylands

125 ml (½ cup) Chicken Bone Broth (page 234)

1 handful of mint leaves

* See Glossary

❶ Toast the coriander seeds, cinnamon, cardamom, cloves, turmeric and cumin seeds in a frying pan over medium heat for 1 minute, tossing occasionally, until fragrant. Grind the toasted spices to a fine powder using a spice grinder or a mortar and pestle.

❷ Drain the soaked chillies and place in the bowl of a food processor, add the shallot, ginger, lemongrass, salt, garlic, honey or sugar, vinegar, oil or fat and ground spices and process to a smooth paste.

❸ Place the chicken pieces in a large bowl, add the spice paste and toss to coat well. Cover and marinate in the fridge for at least 2 hours or, for best results, overnight.

❹ Preheat the oven to 180ºC.

❺ Place the marinated chicken in a roasting tin, spoon the marinade over the top and pour in the broth. Transfer to the oven and roast, basting occasionally, for 35–45 minutes until the chicken is cooked.

❻ Arrange the chicken on a large platter, scatter on the mint leaves and serve.

Over the last ten years I have spent time living and travelling in the USA and have fallen in love with much of their cuisine. And nothing is more flavoursome and unique than the Creole and Cajun dishes from the heart of the Deep South. The iconic and popular gumbo is a meal that you must try at least once in your life – so why not whip up this paleo version at home?

CHICKEN and Sausage GUMBO

SERVES 4

3 tablespoons coconut oil or
    good-quality animal fat*
1 kg chicken thighs (about 4),
    bone in and skin on
sea salt and freshly ground
    black pepper
180 g chorizo or Andouille sausages,
    cut into 2 cm thick slices
100 g speck or rindless bacon,
    chopped into small pieces
30 g (¼ cup) tapioca flour*
1 celery stalk, finely chopped
1 onion, finely chopped
3 garlic cloves, finely chopped
1 red capsicum, finely chopped
2 thyme sprigs
1 teaspoon smoked paprika
pinch of cayenne pepper (optional)
3 × 400 g cans whole peeled tomatoes
    (or 1.2 kg tomatoes, diced)
1 bay leaf
2 pinches of saffron threads
400 ml Chicken Bone Broth
    (page 234)
10 fresh okra pods*
150 g (2 cups) chopped kale or
    spinach
Broccoli Rice (page 232), to serve

See Glossary

❶ Heat the oil or fat in a large, deep frying pan over medium–high heat. Season the chicken with a generous amount of salt and pepper. Working in batches, add the chicken to the pan and cook, skin-side down, until golden brown, 3–4 minutes. Flip the chicken over and cook for 3–4 minutes until golden, then remove from the pan.

❷ Add the sausage and speck or bacon to the pan and cook, stirring occasionally, for 8 minutes until golden brown. Reduce the heat to medium–low, stir in the tapioca flour and cook, stirring constantly, for 30 seconds. Add the celery, onion, garlic and capsicum and cook until the vegetables are soft, about 6 minutes. Add the thyme, smoked paprika, cayenne pepper (if using), tomatoes and bay leaf and cook for 4 minutes.

❸ Return the chicken to the pan, add the saffron, pour in the broth and bring to the boil over high heat.

❹ Reduce the heat to low, cover the pan with a lid and cook for 30 minutes.

❺ Add the okra and kale or spinach to the pan, cover and cook for a further 5 minutes until the chicken is cooked through and the okra is tender. Season with salt and pepper and serve with the broccoli rice on the side.

PRESSURE COOKER Place your pressure cooker over medium heat and follow steps ❶–❷. Follow step ❸, but add only 280 ml of broth rather than 400 ml. Close the lid and lock it, then bring the cooker to high pressure and cook over medium heat to maintain pressure for 15 minutes. Let the pressure drop naturally before opening the lid. Follow step ❺ over medium–high heat.

SLOW COOKER Follow steps ❶–❷, then transfer the ingredients from the pan to your slow cooker. Follow step ❸, but add only 280 ml of broth rather than 400 ml. Cover and cook on high for 2–3 hours until the chicken is cooked through. Mix in the okra and kale or spinach, cover and cook for 15 minutes until the veggies are tender. Season and serve.

BAKED EGGS WITH TOMATO,
ARTICHOKE AND SALAMI *
Porchetta * BRAISED PORK SHANKS
* Pork belly and kimchi stew * STANDING
RIB ROAST PORK WITH RADICCHIO
AND FENNEL * Stuffed bitter melon
with Napoletana sauce * ASIAN-SPICED
ROASTED PORK * Thai pork curry
* HERB-CRUSTED HAM WITH
POMEGRANATE * Pork and cabbage stew

Chapter Four
PORK

A lot of people ask me how salami, bacon and other cured pork products can be paleo. Well, did you know that cured meats are basically fermented? Techniques of preserving meat with salt and spices have been used in cultures around the world for centuries. You may need to hunt around to find good-quality cured products made from free-range pigs – or you could do a workshop to learn how to make them yourself.

Baked EGGS with
SERVES 2   TOMATO, ARTICHOKE AND SALAMI

1 tablespoon coconut oil or
   good-quality animal fat*
½ red onion, sliced
1 × 400 g can diced tomatoes
   (or 400 g tomatoes, diced)
sea salt and freshly ground
   black pepper
8 pitted kalamata olives
1 × 140 g jar marinated artichoke
   hearts, drained and halved
   crossways
50 g salami, sliced
4 eggs
¼ teaspoon chilli flakes (optional)
2 tablespoons chopped mint
1 quarter preserved lemon, flesh
   removed and rind finely sliced

* See Glossary

❶ Preheat the oven to 200°C.

❷ Melt the oil or fat in an ovenproof frying pan over medium heat. Add the onion and cook for 4–5 minutes until soft. Stir in the tomatoes and cook for 10 minutes until slightly reduced. Season with salt and pepper and stir through the olives, artichoke and salami.

❸ Make four indentations in the tomato mixture with the back of a spoon and crack an egg into each. Bake in the oven for 10–15 minutes until the whites have set and the yolks are soft, or cook further to your liking. To finish, sprinkle with the chilli flakes (if using), mint and preserved lemon.

Porchetta is a classic Italian dish of whole roasted pork. A version from Umbria is stuffed – with the pig's chopped entrails that are mixed with lard, garlic, salt, plenty of pepper and wild fennel – and roasted until the skin is crackling and the flesh moist and juicy. The recipe here is a lot simpler: we are simply creating home-style porchetta by flavouring a free-range pork shoulder with spices and seasoning.

SERVES 8

PORCHETTA

2.5 kg boned pork shoulder, skin on

250 ml (1 cup) boiling water

3 tablespoons finely chopped
flat-leaf parsley leaves

1 teaspoon chopped thyme leaves

6 garlic cloves, peeled

1 teaspoon smoked paprika

1 teaspoon chilli flakes (optional)

grated zest of 1 lemon

1 teaspoon freshly crushed black
peppercorns

2 teaspoons fennel seeds, lightly
toasted and crushed

sea salt

2 tablespoons coconut oil or
good-quality animal fat*, melted

See Glossary

❶ Score the skin of the pork shoulder at 2 cm intervals with a sharp knife. Gently pour the boiling water over the pork skin and pat dry with paper towel.

❷ Combine the herbs, garlic, paprika, chilli, lemon zest and peppercorns in the bowl of a food process and process to a coarse paste. Add the fennel seeds and 3 tablespoons of water and continue to process to combine. Season with a little salt.

❸ Preheat the oven to 240ºC.

❹ To butterfly the pork, place the pork, skin-side down, on a chopping board and make a horizontal incision by cutting halfway through the flesh. Open up and flatten the flesh, then spread on the herb mixture. Starting from the long side, tightly roll up the pork, then tie at 5 cm intervals with kitchen string.

❺ Drizzle the oil or fat over the pork skin and rub with 1 tablespoon of salt.

❻ Place the pork in a roasting tin and roast for 35 minutes, or until the skin starts to crackle. Add 125 ml of water to the tin (do not pour it over the crackling), reduce the temperature to 160ºC and cook for a further 2½ hours, or until the juices run clear when a skewer is inserted into the thickest part of the pork. Allow to rest for 15 minutes before carving. Serve with your favourite salad or roasted veggies.

Tip If you find that the pork didn't crackle enough, put it under the grill for 5–8 minutes. Just make sure you keep a close eye on it though, as you don't want it to burn.

I predict in coming years that butchers and online meat suppliers will offer more unique cuts of meat. Here, we braise pork shanks. If you can't find shanks, you could easily replace them with pork belly. The addition of vinegar and wine gives a lovely acidity to this dish and helps balance the richness of the meat. Leftovers can be turned into a soup or shred the meat to add to paleo tacos.

SERVES 6–8

BRAISED PORK *Shanks*

2 pork shanks (about 1 kg each)

sea salt and freshly ground black pepper

3 tablespoons good-quality animal fat*, plus extra if needed

6 French shallots, halved

3 garlic cloves, chopped

3 carrots, chopped

2 tablespoons tomato paste

3 tablespoons apple cider vinegar

250 ml (1 cup) dry white wine

500 g brussels sprouts, trimmed

½ teaspoon chilli flakes (optional)

1 rosemary sprig, leaves picked and roughly chopped

½ teaspoon fennel seeds, toasted

2 teaspoons paprika

200 g canned whole peeled tomatoes, crushed (or 200 g tomatoes, diced)

1.25 litres (5 cups) Chicken Bone Broth (page 234)

2 bay leaves

* See Glossary

❶ Preheat the oven to 150°C.

❷ Season the pork shanks with salt and pepper.

❸ Melt the fat in a large flameproof casserole dish over medium–high heat. Add the pork shanks and cook, turning occasionally, for 6 minutes until golden brown. Remove the shanks from the dish and set aside.

❹ Add more fat if needed to the dish, then add the shallot, garlic and carrot and cook, stirring occasionally, for 5 minutes. Stir in the tomato paste and cook for a further minute until the vegetables are lightly caramelised. Add the vinegar, stir to deglaze and cook until the vinegar has evaporated, 2–3 minutes. Pour in the wine, bring to the boil and simmer until reduced by half, about 5 minutes.

❺ Return the pork shanks to the dish, then add the brussels sprouts, chilli flakes (if using), rosemary, fennel seeds, paprika, tomatoes, broth and bay leaves. Stir and bring to the boil.

❻ Cover with a lid and cook in the oven for 2 hours. Flip the pork shanks in the liquid, add more broth or water if needed, and cook for another 2 hours until the pork is tender and falling off the bone.

❼ Remove the shanks and vegetables from the braising liquid with tongs. Transfer to a serving platter, cover and keep warm. Place the dish with the braising liquid on the stovetop and simmer until reduced by half, about 15 minutes. Spoon the braising juices over the pork and vegetables and serve.

PRESSURE COOKER Follow step ❷. Using your pressure cooker over medium–high heat, follow steps ❸–❹. Follow step ❺, adding only 800 ml of broth rather than 1.25 litres. Close and lock the lid, then bring the cooker to high pressure and cook over medium heat for 45 minutes. Let the pressure drop naturally before opening the lid. Follow step ❼.

SLOW COOKER Follow steps ❷–❹, then transfer all the ingredients from the casserole dish to your slow cooker. Follow step ❺, cover with the lid and cook on low for 10–12 hours. Follow step ❼, transferring the braising liquid to a saucepan to reduce it by half.

I am a huge fan of Korean food, especially their health-giving kimchi, a fermented vegetable side dish that is a staple in all Korean homes, much like sauerkraut is for a lot of Europeans. The healthy bacteria present in the kimchi will most likely be destroyed by the heat when you stir it through the stew at the end, so make sure you serve some extra kimchi on the side for good gut health.

PORK BELLY
SERVES 4 and Kimchi Stew

3 tablespoons tamari or coconut
   aminos*
1 tablespoon sesame oil
1 tablespoon finely grated ginger
1 teaspoon honey
1 kg boned pork belly, cut into
   2.5 cm dice
2 tablespoons coconut oil or
   good-quality animal fat*
8 shiitake mushrooms
6 garlic cloves, finely chopped
3 spring onions, finely sliced, plus
   extra to serve
750 ml (3 cups) Chicken Bone Broth
   (page 234)
½ teaspoon Korean chilli powder
   (gochugaru)*
½ carrot, coarsely grated
300 g kimchi (for a recipe, see
   page 238), drained and roughly
   chopped, plus extra to serve
sea salt and freshly ground
   black pepper

* See Glossary

❶ Place the tamari or coconut aminos, sesame oil, ginger and honey in a large bowl, add the pork and toss to coat. Cover with plastic wrap and marinate for 1 hour in the fridge. Strain the meat, reserving the marinade.

❷ Melt the coconut oil or fat in a large frying pan over medium–high heat. Add the pork belly and cook, turning occasionally, for 5 minutes until browned. Add the mushrooms, garlic and spring onion and sauté until softened, 1–2 minutes.

❸ Pour the reserved marinade and the broth into the pan, then add the chilli powder and bring to the boil.

❹ Reduce the heat to low, cover and simmer gently until the pork belly is tender, 35–40 minutes.

❺ Remove from the heat. Add the carrot and kimchi to the stew, stir and season to taste. Serve with the extra spring onion scattered on top and some more kimchi on the side.

PRESSURE COOKER Follow step ❶. Using your pressure cooker over medium–high heat, follow step ❷. Follow step ❸, but add only 520 ml of broth rather than 750 ml. Close and lock the lid, then bring the cooker to high pressure and cook over medium heat for 20 minutes. Let the pressure drop naturally before opening the lid. Follow step ❺.

SLOW COOKER Follow steps ❶–❷, then transfer the browned pork and all the ingredients from the pan to your slow cooker. Follow step ❸, but add only 520 ml of broth rather than 750 ml. Cover and cook on low for 8–10 hours. Follow step ❺.

A special occasion calls for a special meal. And what could be more special than a scrumptious roast rack of pork with crackling, sweet apples, bitter radicchio, aniseed-flavoured fennel and just a touch of chilli for good measure? Serve with a glorious fresh leaf salad and some beautiful sauerkraut on the side and you will be in culinary heaven.

Standing Rib ROAST PORK

WITH RADICCHIO AND FENNEL

SERVES 4–6

2 teaspoons fennel seeds,
   lightly toasted
2 teaspoons sea salt
250 ml (1 cup) boiling water
1.2 kg rack of pork, skin on
2 tablespoons coconut oil or
   good-quality animal fat*, melted
2 garlic cloves, finely chopped
4 tablespoons maple syrup
3 tablespoons lemon juice
1 teaspoon chilli flakes
1 large radicchio, cut into quarters
   lengthways
2 fennel bulbs, cut into quarters
1 apple, cut in half lengthways
freshly ground black pepper

* See Glossary

❶ Preheat the oven to 230°C. Grease a roasting tin.

❷ Using a mortar and pestle, grind the fennel seeds into a coarse powder, then mix in the salt. Set aside.

❸ Gently pour the boiling water over the pork skin and pat dry with paper towel. Score the skin along the length of the rib lines with a sharp knife. Place the pork rack in the prepared roasting tin. Drizzle the oil or fat over the pork skin and rub with the fennel seed mixture, covering the skin and the meat evenly. Roast in the oven for 30 minutes.

❹ Meanwhile, combine the garlic, maple syrup, lemon juice and half the chilli flakes in a large bowl and mix well. Add the radicchio, fennel and apple and gently toss. Season with salt and pepper.

❺ Reduce the oven temperature to 180°C and roast the pork rack for a further 20 minutes. Remove half of the juices collected in the base of the tin and arrange the fennel, apple and radicchio around the pork. Return to the oven to roast for 20 minutes until cooked through. (You can check to see if it's cooked through by inserting a thermometer – when it reaches 68–71°C, it's ready.)

❻ Remove the pork rack from the oven, sprinkle on the remaining chilli flakes and transfer to a warm platter to rest for 10–15 minutes. Turn the apple, fennel, and radicchio in the tin and return to the oven to roast for a further 15 minutes until tender and caramelised.

❼ To serve, slice the pork rack between the ribs into portions and chop the apple into large pieces. Serve the pork with the roast radicchio, fennel and apple.

This unusual dish may not suit everyone's palate – bitter melon is, as its name suggests, quite bitter. What I love, though, is how simple and delicious this is. Basically, it is a pimped up meatball dish. If you can't find bitter melon or don't like the flavour, you can swap it for some hollowed out zucchini boats or fill some mushrooms or capsicums with the mixture.

Stuffed Bitter Melon

SERVES 4 **WITH NAPOLETANA SAUCE**

3 bitter melons*
500 g pork mince
2 garlic cloves, finely chopped
1 handful of flat-leaf parsley
    leaves, chopped
1 egg
sea salt and freshly ground
    black pepper
2 tablespoons coconut oil or
    good-quality animal fat*
1–2 macadamia nuts (activated if
    possible*), finely grated
1 small handful of basil leaves

Napoletana sauce
2 tablespoons coconut oil or
    good-quality animal fat*, melted
1 onion, finely chopped
4 garlic cloves, finely sliced
2 salted anchovy fillets, rinsed and
    patted dry (optional)
1–2 long red chillies, deseeded and
    finely sliced
3 tablespoons chopped flat-leaf
    parsley leaves
1 × 400 g can whole peeled tomatoes,
    crushed (or 400 g tomatoes,
    diced)
125 ml (½ cup) Chicken Bone Broth
    (page 234)
sea salt and freshly ground
    black pepper

* See Glossary

❶ Slice the bitter melons into 3 cm thick rings. Remove and discard the inner core from each slice. Set aside.

❷ Combine the pork, garlic, parsley and egg in a bowl, season with salt and pepper and mix well. Spoon 1½ tablespoons of the filling into the centre of each bitter melon ring, pressing with your hands to firmly pack in the filling.

❸ Melt the oil or fat in a large, deep frying pan over medium heat. Add the filled melon rings in batches and cook on each side for 2 minutes until golden. Remove from the pan and set aside.

❹ To make the sauce, heat the oil or fat in the pan over medium heat, add the onion and cook for 5 minutes until translucent. Stir in the garlic and anchovies (if using) and cook until the garlic starts to turn golden, about 30 seconds. Add the chilli and parsley and toss for 20 seconds. Pour in the tomatoes and broth and season with salt and pepper. Return the melon to the pan in a single layer. Cover with a lid, reduce the heat to medium–low and simmer for 15–20 minutes until the melon is cooked through.

❺ Spoon the melon and sauce onto a platter and scatter the grated macadamias and the basil leaves over the top.

Ask any chef what their favourite animal to cook with is and nine times out of ten they will say pasture raised pork. Why? Well, I think it is all about the amount of fat and the versatility of the different cuts, which allow the whole animal to be used in culinary preparations. Here we have a delicious Asian-inspired roasted pork shoulder that will sing on your palate and be a welcome addition to your weekly roast dinner.

Asian-spiced ROASTED PORK

SERVES 6–8

2 kg boneless pork shoulder,
    skin left on

3 tablespoons Paleo Hoisin Sauce
    (page 240)

1½ teaspoons sea salt

2 tablespoons tamari or coconut
    aminos*

1 litre (4 cups) Chicken Bone Broth
    (page 234)

5 cm piece of ginger, sliced

4 long red chillies

3 star anise

3 tablespoons coconut sugar

Spice mix

1½ tablespoons Sichuan
    peppercorns

6 star anise

4 whole cloves

½ cinnamon stick

1½ teaspoons fennel seeds

5 whole allspice berries

½ teaspoon dried chilli flakes

1 teaspoon sea salt

See Glossary

❶ To make the spice mix, place the peppercorns, star anise, cloves, cinnamon, fennel seeds, allspice and chilli flakes in a small frying pan over medium heat and cook, tossing frequently, for 2 minutes until fragrant. Remove from the tin and allow to cool. Use a spice grinder or mortar and pestle to grind the spices to a fine powder, then mix in the salt.

❷ Preheat the oven to 150°C.

❸ Using a sharp knife, score the pork skin at 5 cm intervals. Rub the hoisin sauce all over the pork flesh to evenly coat (don't rub it on the skin). Then rub 3½ tablespoons of the spice mix over the pork flesh only. Rub the salt on the skin.

❹ Combine the remaining ingredients in the roasting tin and set over medium heat on the stovetop. Bring to the boil, then remove from the heat. Place the pork, skin-side up, in the tin. Tightly cover the tin with two layers of foil and transfer to the oven to cook for 2½ hours until the pork is cooked through and tender. Increase the oven temperature to 230°C, remove the foil and roast the pork for a further 30 minutes to crisp the skin. Reserve the stock for other cooking or reduce it to make a sauce.

Tip Store the leftover spice mix in an airtight container for up to 3 months in the pantry.

I love to slowly simmer pork to develop the flavour and allow the meat to become increasingly tender. Here, the pork's done in a fragrant Thai red curry sauce. I usually make up a big batch, so we can eat the curry for days, or freeze some for later. Feel free to play around with different vegetables that are in season. The wonderful thing about curries is they suit all climates and all times of the year.

SERVES 6

Thai PORK CURRY

4 tablespoons coconut oil or good-quality animal fat*

1 kg pork shoulder, cut into 2 cm pieces

8 red Asian shallots, finely chopped

4 garlic cloves, chopped

2 tablespoons finely grated ginger

3 tablespoons Thai red curry paste (for a recipe, see page 243)

1 × 400 ml can coconut cream

500 ml (2 cups) Chicken Bone Broth (page 234)

2 kaffir lime leaves, torn

6 Japanese eggplants, cut into 2 cm thick slices

2 long red chillies, cut in half lengthways and deseeded (optional)

splash of fish sauce

1½ tablespoons coconut sugar

1½ tablespoons tamarind puree*

1 large handful of coriander leaves, to serve

Broccoli or Cauliflower Rice (pages 232 and 233), to serve

See Glossary

❶ Heat half the oil or fat in a heavy-based saucepan over high heat. Working in batches, add the pork and fry, turning occasionally, for 4 minutes until the meat is lightly browned. Remove the pork from the pan and set aside.

❷ Reduce the heat to medium, add the remaining oil or fat and the shallot to the pan and sauté for 5 minutes until the shallot is translucent. Stir in the garlic, ginger and curry paste and cook for 1 minute until fragrant.

❸ Return the pork to the pan, then stir in the coconut cream, broth and lime leaves and bring to the boil.

❹ Reduce the heat to low, cover the pan with a lid and cook for 1 hour.

❺ Add the eggplant and chilli (if using) to the curry and stir.

❻ Cover and gently simmer the curry for a further hour until the pork is very tender.

❼ Stir the fish sauce into the curry, add the coconut sugar and tamarind puree, then taste. There should be a pronounced tartness with a balance of sweetness – adjust the seasoning if necessary.

❽ Sprinkle over the coriander and serve with the broccoli or cauliflower rice.

PRESSURE COOKER Using your pressure cooker over medium heat, follow steps ❶–❷. Follow step ❸, but add only 350 ml of broth rather than 500 ml. Close and lock the lid, then bring the cooker to high pressure and cook over medium heat for 20 minutes. Let the pressure drop naturally before opening the lid. Follow step ❺, close and lock the lid. Bring the cooker to high pressure and cook over medium–low heat for 5 minutes. Let the pressure drop naturally before opening the lid. Follow steps ❼–❽.

SLOW COOKER Follow steps ❶–❷, then transfer the ingredients from the pan to your slow cooker. Follow step ❸, but add only 350 ml of broth rather than 500 ml. Cover and cook on low for 6 hours. Follow step ❺, cover and cook on low for 2 hours, then follow steps ❼–❽.

I do love a Christmas ham and I am always looking for ways to jazz it up. Searching for inspiration around the world, I remembered the intoxicating flavour of pomegranate molasses, and thought how wonderful that would be cooked into a gorgeous leg of ham that is then topped with an acidic tahini dressing and an abundance of fresh herbs, walnuts and pomegranate seeds.

Herb-crusted HAM with POMEGRANATE

SERVES 15–20

1 × 5 kg leg of ham
seeds of 1 pomegranate, to serve

Glaze
3 tablespoons pomegranate
    molasses*
3 tablespoons honey

Tahini dressing
350 g unhulled tahini
100 ml lemon juice
1 teaspoon ground cumin
2 garlic cloves, finely chopped

Herb crust
1 red onion, finely chopped
2 very large handfuls of coriander
    leaves, finely chopped
2 large handfuls of flat-leaf parsley
    leaves, finely chopped
1 large handful of mint leaves,
    finely chopped
2 long red chillies, finely chopped
    (optional)
200 g walnuts (activated if
    possible*), toasted and finely
    chopped
2 tablespoons sumac*

See Glossary

❶ Preheat the oven to 160°C.

❷ To prepare the ham, lift off the skin and score a diamond pattern into the fat. (This allows the flavours of the glaze to penetrate the meat.)

❸ To make the glaze, combine the pomegranate molasses and honey with 3 tablespoons of water in a bowl and mix well.

❹ Using a pastry brush, spread just enough glaze over the ham to cover. Reserve the remaining glaze for basting. Place the ham in a roasting tin and pour in water to a depth of 2 cm. Bake in the oven for 1–1½ hours, basting with the reserved glaze from time to time. (Loosely cover with foil if it is beginning to burn.) Remove from the oven, cover with foil and set aside in a warm place to rest for 15 minutes.

❺ To make the tahini dressing, place all the ingredients in the bowl of a food processor, add 240 ml of water and process to form a thick sauce.

❻ To make the herb crust, combine all the ingredients in a bowl.

❼ Transfer the ham to a large serving platter. Spread the tahini dressing on top, cover with the herb crust and sprinkle on the pomegranate seeds. Slice the ham and serve with some kraut (for a recipe, see page 231) or a fresh salad.

European slow-cooked stews are so comforting, and I find they are a great first step in getting kids to be more adventurous with their food. From there you can expand their palates and introduce them to and explore the wonderful spicy dishes from Asian cultures. Pork shoulder, cabbage, porcini mushrooms, bone broth, spinach and apples, to name just a few ingredients, are combined in this super nutrient-dense dish.

PORK and CABBAGE Stew

SERVES 4

10 g (1 heaped tablespoon) dried porcini mushrooms

250 ml (1 cup) boiling water

2 tablespoons coconut oil or good-quality animal fat*

150 g pancetta, cut into 1 cm cubes

1 kg boned pork shoulder, cut into 2.5 cm cubes

2 onions, roughly chopped

4 garlic cloves, finely chopped

1 teaspoon caraway seeds

1 teaspoon ground allspice

1 teaspoon smoked paprika

100 g tomato paste

500 g green cabbage, finely shredded

625 ml (2½ cups) Chicken Bone Broth (page 234)

125 ml (½ cup) dry white wine

2 bay leaves

sea salt and freshly ground black pepper

2 pink lady apples, peeled, cored and chopped

2 large handfuls of baby spinach

sage leaves, to serve

* See Glossary

❶ Place the dried porcini mushrooms in a bowl, cover with the boiling water and leave to soak for 20 minutes until softened. Strain, reserving the liquid, and roughly chop the mushrooms. Set aside.

❷ Melt 1 tablespoon of the oil or fat in a heavy-based saucepan over medium–high heat, add the pancetta and fry until golden brown, about 5 minutes. Remove the pancetta with a slotted spoon.

❸ Working in batches, add the pork to the pan and cook for 6–8 minutes until golden brown on all sides. Remove from the pan and set aside. Reduce the heat to medium, add the remaining oil or fat and the onion and cook, stirring occasionally, for 5 minutes until soft. Stir in the garlic, caraway seeds, allspice, paprika and tomato paste and cook for 1 minute until fragrant. Return the pancetta and pork to the pan.

❹ Mix in the cabbage, the reserved porcini water and porcini, the broth, wine and bay leaves and season with salt and pepper.

❺ Bring to the boil, then reduce the heat to low and simmer for 2 hours.

❻ Stir the apple into the stew and cook for 30 minutes until the meat is very tender.

❼ Add the spinach to the stew, stir, sprinkle on some sage and serve.

PRESSURE COOKER Follow step ❶. Using your pressure cooker over medium–high heat, follow steps ❷–❸. Follow step ❹, but add only 375 ml of broth rather than 625 ml. Close the lid and lock it, then bring the cooker to high pressure and cook over medium heat for 30 minutes. Let the pressure drop naturally before opening the lid. Stir in the apple and cook, uncovered, for 15 minutes over medium–low heat, stirring occasionally. Follow step ❼.

SLOW COOKER Follow steps ❶–❸, then transfer the pork, pancetta and all the ingredients from the pan to your slow cooker. Follow step ❹, but add only 375 ml of broth rather than 625 ml. Cover and cook on low for 8 hours until tender. Add the apple, cover and continue to cook on low for 1½ hours. Follow step ❼.

Braised lamb with Jerusalem artichokes
* JAMAICAN GOAT CURRY *
Baked eggs with lamb kofta * BRAISED
RABBIT HOTPOT * Moroccan-spiced
leg of lamb with roasted fennel *
BRAISED GOAT SHANKS WITH
MINT PISTOU * Lamb liver masala *
MIDDLE EASTERN LAMB STEW
* Lazy man's lamb shoulder *
GOAT CASSEROLE * Chilli venison stew
* LAMB KOFTA CURRY * Brain curry
* LAMB SHANK HARIRA * Rabbit stew

Chapter Five
LAMB, GOAT
& GAME

Is there a more magnificent pairing than cumin and lamb? Whether it is a simple lamb burger patty with ground cumin or a braised lamb shoulder with cumin seeds, the flavour combination creates lasting memories. Here, we have teamed lamb and cumin with some Jerusalem artichokes, one of my all-time favourite ingredients. If you can't find Jerusalem artichokes, use sweet potatoes, turnips, parsnips or fennel.

Braised LAMB

SERVES 4–6 WITH JERUSALEM ARTICHOKES

2.4 kg lamb leg (bone in), cut into 12 cm pieces (ask your butcher to do this)

1 teaspoon cumin seeds

sea salt and freshly ground black pepper

1 tablespoon coconut oil or good-quality animal fat*

1 large onion, roughly chopped

3 carrots, roughly chopped

2 celery stalks, roughly chopped

6 garlic cloves, roughly chopped

250 ml (1 cup) dry white wine

185 ml (¾ cup) Chicken Bone Broth (page 234)

3 rosemary sprigs, leaves picked

2 bay leaves

1 teaspoon celery seeds

4 parsnips, chopped into thirds

4 Jerusalem artichokes, halved

* See Glossary

❶ Preheat the oven to 90°C or the lowest setting.

❷ Score the fat of the lamb and rub the cumin seeds and salt and pepper into the score marks.

❸ Melt the oil or fat in a large flameproof casserole dish over medium–high heat, add the lamb in batches and brown on all sides for 3–5 minutes. Remove from the dish and place, fat-side up, on a plate.

❹ Add the onion to the dish and cook, stirring occasionally, for 2–4 minutes until softened. Add the carrot, celery and garlic and cook until starting to colour, 2–4 minutes.

❺ Stir the wine, broth, herbs and celery seeds into the dish, bring to the boil, season with salt and pepper, then return the browned lamb.

❻ Add the parsnip and Jerusalem artichoke to the dish.

❼ Cover the dish with a lid or tightly seal with foil and braise in the oven for 10–11 hours until the lamb pulls apart easily. Serve with a crisp green salad.

PRESSURE COOKER Follow step ❷. Using your pressure cooker over medium heat, follow steps ❸–❹. Follow steps ❺–❻, close the lid and lock it, then bring the cooker to high pressure and cook over medium–low heat for 45 minutes. Let the pressure drop naturally before opening the lid.

SLOW COOKER Follow steps ❷–❻, then transfer the browned lamb and ingredients to your slow cooker. Cover with the lid and cook on low for 10–11 hours, or until the meat is tender.

Using spices should be an integral part of everyone's cooking. If your spice cabinet is looking bare, I encourage you to buy a different spice every week, research it and find a recipe to use it in. At the end of the year you'll be very well educated about spices – and you'll have some great new recipes, too. If you can't find goat, or the family isn't keen on it, simply use lamb.

SERVES 4–6

Jamaican GOAT CURRY

1 kg boned goat (or lamb) shoulder, cut into 5 cm pieces
4 tablespoons coconut oil or good-quality animal fat*, melted
sea salt and freshly ground black pepper
1 onion, chopped
1 habanero chilli, deseeded and finely chopped
4 garlic cloves, finely chopped
1 teaspoon finely grated ginger
1 × 400 ml can coconut milk
500 ml (2 cups) Beef or Chicken Bone Broth (pages 230 and 234)
1 × 400 g can whole peeled tomatoes, crushed (or 400 g tomatoes, diced)
1 teaspoon thyme leaves
1 sweet potato (about 300 g), cut into 2.5 cm pieces
12 fresh okra pods*, cut in half
Cauliflower Rice (page 233), to serve

Jamaican curry powder
3 tablespoons coriander seeds
2 tablespoons cumin seeds
2 tablespoons yellow mustard seeds
2 star anise
1 tablespoon fenugreek seeds
1 tablespoon whole allspice berries
5 tablespoons ground turmeric

* See Glossary

❶ To make the Jamaican curry powder, combine all the ingredients except the turmeric in a heavy-based saucepan and toast over medium heat until fragrant, 1–2 minutes. Grind the spices in a spice grinder, add the turmeric and mix well.

❷ Pat the goat dry with paper towel and place in a bowl. Add 2 tablespoons of the oil or fat and 2 tablespoons of the curry powder and season with salt and pepper. Toss gently to coat, cover with plastic wrap and marinate in the fridge for 1 hour.

❸ Heat 1 tablespoon of the oil or fat in the pan over medium heat. Add the goat in batches and cook for 6 minutes until well browned on all sides. Set aside.

❹ Wipe the pan clean. Heat the remaining oil or fat over medium heat, add the onion and chilli and sauté until just starting to colour, about 5 minutes. Stir in the garlic, ginger and 2 tablespoons of the curry powder and sauté for 1–2 minutes. (Leftover curry powder can be stored in a jar in the pantry for up to 3 months.)

❺ Return the meat to the pan and add the coconut milk, broth, tomatoes and thyme. Season with salt and pepper and bring to the boil.

❻ Reduce the heat to low, cover with the lid and simmer gently for 2 hours.

❼ Stir the sweet potato into the curry, cover and cook for 30 minutes.

❽ Add the okra to the curry and cook for 10 minutes until the meat and vegetables are tender. Skim off any fat, season and serve with cauliflower rice.

PRESSURE COOKER Follow steps ❶–❷. Using your pressure cooker over medium–high heat, follow steps ❸–❹. Follow step ❺, but add only 350 ml of broth rather than 500 ml. Close and lock the lid, then bring to high pressure and cook over medium heat for 25 minutes. Let the pressure drop naturally before opening the lid. Add the sweet potato, close and lock the lid, then bring to high pressure and cook over medium heat for 5 minutes. Let the pressure drop naturally before opening the lid. Follow step ❽.

SLOW COOKER Follow steps ❶–❹. Transfer everything in the pan to your slow cooker. Add the meat, coconut milk, 350 ml of broth, tomatoes and thyme, cover and cook on low for 8–10 hours. Add the sweet potato and okra and cook, uncovered, on high for 1 hour until tender. Skim, season and serve.

When people ask about my favourite breakfast dishes, I often mention these baked eggs – but there is no reason they can't be enjoyed at any time of the day or night. I love that a lot of the elements in this recipe can be made ahead of time, so you can just bang everything together at the last minute. Always make a double or triple batch, as this is awesome cold the next day. Serve with a salad and some fermented veg.

Baked EGGS
SERVES 4 *with* LAMB KOFTA

500 g lamb mince
1 garlic clove, finely chopped
1 teaspoon pomegranate molasses*
2 tablespoons chopped flat-leaf
　　parsley leaves
1 tablespoon Turkish Spice Blend
　　(page 244)
sea salt and freshly ground
　　black pepper
2 tablespoons coconut oil or
　　good-quality animal fat*
1 large handful of baby spinach
　　leaves
4 eggs

Sauce
2 tablespoons coconut oil or good-
　　quality animal fat*
2 onions, finely chopped
2 garlic cloves, finely chopped
2 × 400 g cans diced tomatoes
　　(or 800 g tomatoes, diced)
1 teaspoon ground cumin
½ teaspoon ground cinnamon
1–2 pinches of cayenne pepper
400 ml Beef Bone Broth (page 230)
　　or water

To serve
4 tablespoons Chermoula (page 233)
4 tablespoons coconut yoghurt
　　(for a recipe, see page 235)
1–2 pinches of sumac*
baby coriander leaves

* See Glossary

❶ Combine the lamb, garlic, pomegranate molasses, parsley, spice blend and salt and pepper in a bowl and mix well. With wet hands, shape the mixture into walnut-sized kofta.

❷ Melt the oil or fat in a large flameproof casserole dish over medium–high heat. Add the kofta and seal for 2–3 minutes until brown all over. Remove from the dish and drain on paper towel.

❸ Preheat the oven to 180°C.

❹ To make the sauce, melt the oil or fat in the dish over medium heat. Add the onion and garlic and sauté for 5 minutes until soft and translucent. Stir in the tomatoes, cumin, cinnamon and cayenne pepper and season with salt and pepper. Pour in the broth or water, stir well and bring to the boil. Reduce the heat to low and simmer for 30 minutes until reduced and thick.

❺ Gently stir the kofta into the sauce and cook for 5 minutes. Stir through the spinach. Make four indentations in the sauce and crack an egg into each one. (Alternatively, if you prefer to make individual servings, transfer the meatballs and sauce to four small ovenproof dishes, make an indentation in the centre and crack in an egg.) Season with salt and pepper, cover with the lid and bake in the oven for 10–12 minutes until the eggs are just cooked. Remove from the oven, drizzle over the chermoula and yoghurt, then sprinkle on some sumac and baby coriander.

It is amazing how good braised rabbit can taste, especially when you add an array of wonderful spices that meld together and permeate the flesh with flavour. Here, we use a combination of cinnamon, ginger, coriander seeds and star anise to make the rabbit shine. You can swap out the rabbit and use chicken marylands or pork belly if you like.

SERVES 4

Braised RABBIT HOTPOT

4 garlic cloves, finely chopped

1 teaspoon finely grated ginger

100 ml dry white wine

500 ml (2 cups) Chicken Bone Broth (page 234)

1 cinnamon stick

2 star anise

½ teaspoon coriander seeds, toasted and lightly crushed

¼ teaspoon celery seeds

6 thyme sprigs

1 tablespoon apple cider vinegar

1 rabbit (about 1.5 kg) with liver, cut into 8 pieces (ask you butcher to do this)

sea salt and freshly ground black pepper

2 tablespoons coconut oil or good-quality animal fat*

2 onions, sliced

6 tomatoes, cut into large pieces or quarters

2 turnips, cut into 3 cm pieces

juice of ½ lemon

1 handful of coriander and flat-leaf parsley leaves, chopped

* See Glossary

❶ Place the garlic, ginger, wine, broth, cinmmon, star anise, coriander seeds, celery seeds, thyme and vinegar in a large non-reactive dish and mix well. Add the rabbit pieces and the liver, cover with plastic wrap and refrigerate for 8 hours or overnight.

❷ Remove the rabbit pieces and liver and reserve the marinade. Pat the rabbit dry with paper towel, then season with salt and pepper.

❸ Preheat the oven to 150°C.

❹ Melt the oil or fat in a flameproof casserole dish over high heat and add the rabbit. Cook for 4 minutes until golden brown on each side, then remove from the dish.

❺ Reduce the heat to medium, add the onion and cook, stirring occasionally, for 5 minutes until soft. Add the tomato, turnip and reserved marinade and stir well. Return the rabbit to the dish, add the liver and bring to the boil.

❻ Cover the dish with the lid and transfer to the oven. Cook for 2 hours until the rabbit is tender. Stir in the lemon juice, season with salt and pepper, scatter on the herbs and serve.

PRESSURE COOKER Follow steps ❶–❷, adding only 350 ml of broth rather than 500 ml. Using your pressure cooker over medium–high heat, follow steps ❹–❺. Close the lid and lock it, then bring the cooker to high pressure and cook over medium heat for 15 minutes. Let the pressure drop naturally before opening the lid. Season, scatter on the herbs and serve.

SLOW COOKER Follow steps ❶–❷, adding only 350 ml of broth rather than 500 ml. Follow steps ❹–❺, then transfer all the ingredients from the casserole dish to your slow cooker. Cover and cook on low for 6–8 hours. Season, scatter on the herbs and serve.

How impressive is a beautifully roasted leg of lamb on the dinner table? And it is even better when cooked with the most tantalising Moroccan spices that flood the kitchen and dining room with their warming aromas. This is lovely with a fresh salad on the side and some fermented veg as well.

Moroccan-spiced LEG of LAMB
SERVES 6 WITH ROASTED FENNEL

1 × 2.5 kg leg of lamb
6 garlic cloves, peeled
2 large fennel bulbs, cut into quarters
1 large onion, sliced into 1 cm thick rings
8 thyme sprigs
500 ml (2 cups) Beef or Chicken Bone Broth (pages 230 and 234)
sea salt

Spice paste
2 tablespoons coriander seeds
2 tablespoons cumin seeds
3 teaspoons paprika
2 teaspoons freshly ground black pepper
1½ teaspoons sea salt
¼ teaspoon cayenne pepper
2 teaspoons dried mint
6 garlic cloves, finely chopped
4 tablespoons lemon juice
3 tablespoons coconut oil or good-quality animal fat*, melted

See Glossary

❶ Preheat the oven to 180°C. Grease a large roasting tin.

❷ To make the spice paste, coarsely grind the coriander and cumin seeds using a mortar and pestle or spice grinder. Transfer to a bowl, add the remaining ingredients and mix to form a paste. Set aside until needed.

❸ Using the tip of a sharp knife, make 5 mm deep incisions all over the lamb.

❹ Scatter the garlic, fennel, onion and thyme in the base of the prepared tin. Sit the lamb on top and rub the spice paste evenly over the surface.

❺ Pour 250 ml of the broth into the spice paste bowl to remove any remaining paste, then pour over the lamb. Place in the oven and roast, basting the lamb occasionally with the juices that collect in the tin, for 1½ hours. If you prefer your lamb well done, cook for a further 15 minutes.

❻ Remove the lamb from the tin and place on a carving board, cover loosely with foil and allow to rest for 15 minutes. Transfer the vegetables from the tin to a serving dish and cover to keep warm.

❼ Place the tin over medium heat on the stovetop, pour in the remaining broth and bring to the boil. Using a wooden spoon, stir to dislodge any cooked-on bits, and cook until reduced by two-thirds and a sauce-like consistency. Season with salt if needed.

❽ Carve the lamb and serve with the roasted vegetables and lamb jus.

This is a wonderfully aromatic and gentle recipe of braised goat shanks that will leave you wanting more. It will also confirm why goat is the world's most consumed meat, as – if you know how to cook it – it is simply delicious. The addition of the mint pistou elevates this meal to another level. You can swap out the goat for lamb, chicken or pork.

Braised GOAT SHANKS
SERVES 4   WITH MINT PISTOU

4 goat (or lamb) shanks (about
    500 g each)
sea salt and freshly ground
    black pepper
2 tablespoons duck fat
4 garlic cloves, chopped
2 celery stalks, finely chopped
1 onion, finely chopped
2 carrots, finely chopped
1.25 litres (5 cups) Chicken Bone
    Broth (page 234)
8 thyme sprigs
1 rosemary sprig
2 bay leaves
¼ teaspoon black peppercorns

Mint pistou
1 large handful of flat-leaf parsley
    leaves
2 large handfuls of mint leaves
40 g (scant ⅓ cup) pistachio nuts
    (activated if possible*), toasted
½ teaspoon ground cumin
2 tablespoons lemon juice
100 ml extra-virgin olive oil

* See Glossary

❶ Preheat the oven to 160°C.

❷ Season the shanks with salt and pepper.

❸ Melt the fat in a large flameproof casserole dish over high heat. Add the shanks and brown on all sides for 5 minutes until golden, then remove from the heat.

❹ Add the remaining ingredients to the dish and stir through.

❺ Cover the dish with the lid, place in the oven and cook for 3 hours until the meat is falling off the bone.

❻ Remove the shanks from the dish. Place the dish on the stovetop over medium–high heat and cook until the braising liquid is reduced by half, about 20 minutes. Return the shanks to the dish to gently reheat for 10 minutes.

❼ Meanwhile, to make the mint pistou, place all the ingredients in the bowl of a food processor and whiz until finely chopped. Season with salt and pepper.

❽ Remove the shanks from the braising liquid and place in bowls. Ladle over the veggie broth, then spoon some mint pistou over the top.

PRESSURE COOKER Follow step ❷. Using your pressure cooker over high heat, follow step ❸. Follow step ❹, close and lock the lid, then bring the cooker to high pressure and cook over medium heat for 45 minutes. Let the pressure drop naturally before opening the lid. Remove the shanks and cook the braising liquid, uncovered, over high heat for 20 minutes. Return the shanks to the braising liquid, reduce the heat to low and gently reheat for 10 minutes. Follow steps ❼–❽.

SLOW COOKER Follow step ❷–❸. Using your slow cooker, follow step ❹, cover with the lid and cook on low for 8–10 hours. Follow step ❻ and reduce the braising liquid by half in a large saucepan. Then follow steps ❼–❽.

Indian offal dishes are some of the most tantalising in the world. If you are a bit squeamish when it comes to offal, I recommend trying it in a preparation like this, as the spices really add to the amazing lusciousness of the liver. If you really cannot get your head wrapped around eating liver, you can try using lamb loin and prepare and cook it the same way until it is pink and tender.

SERVES 4

Lamb Liver MASALA

4 tablespoons coconut oil or good-quality animal fat*

800 g lamb liver, trimmed and cut into 2 cm cubes (or you could use chicken livers if you prefer)

2 large onions, chopped

3 garlic cloves, finely chopped

1 tablespoon finely chopped coriander leaves, plus extra leaves to serve

1 long red chilli, deseeded and finely chopped

½ teaspoon ground turmeric

2 teaspoons ground coriander

1 teaspoon ground cumin

pinch of cayenne pepper

4 long red chillies (optional)

250 ml (1 cup) Beef or Chicken Bone Broth (pages 230 and 234) or water

sea salt and freshly ground black pepper

juice of ½ lime

Cauliflower Rice (page 233), to serve

See Glossary

❶ Melt 1 tablespoon of the oil or fat in a large frying pan over medium–high heat. Add the liver in batches and seal for 30 seconds each side until golden brown. Set aside. Wipe the pan clean, then add the remaining oil or fat and the onion and cook over medium heat for 5 minutes until translucent. Stir in the garlic, chopped coriander and chopped chilli and fry for 1 minute until the garlic is soft.

❷ Add the spices and whole chillies (if using) to the pan and cook, stirring occasionally, for 1 minute until fragrant.

❸ Add the liver, pour in the broth or water, stir well, then bring to a simmer and cook for 5 minutes until the liver is slightly pink in the middle. Season with salt and pepper.

❹ Stir in the lime juice, sprinkle the extra coriander leaves over the liver masala and serve with cauliflower rice.

This stew uses the Arabic spice blend baharat, which makes nearly every protein dance on your tastebuds. An all-round mix that changes from region to region and household to household, baharat always includes black pepper, cumin, cinnamon and cloves, as well as a host of other spices. If you want an adventurous dish for your next family dinner that will have them asking for more, then give this a try.

Middle Eastern LAMB STEW

SERVES 4

2 teaspoons sea salt

1 large eggplant, halved lengthways and cut into 1 cm thick slices

900 g boned lamb shoulder, cut into 2.5 cm cubes

3 teaspoons ground coriander

2 teaspoons baharat* or garam masala

1 teaspoon ground cumin

freshly ground black pepper

2 tablespoons coconut oil or good-quality animal fat*

1 large onion, chopped

3 garlic cloves, chopped

1 long red chilli, deseeded and finely chopped (leave the seeds in if you like it spicy)

2 carrots, chopped

1 large turnip, cut into 2 cm chucks

4 tablespoons pomegranate molasses*

2 bay leaves

1 handful of coriander and mint leaves, roughly chopped

Cauliflower Rice (page 233), to serve

See Glossary

❶ Place the salt in a bowl, pour in 1 litre of water and stir to dissolve. Add the eggplant, cover with a small plate to keep the eggplant submerged and allow to soak for 30 minutes. Drain and pat dry with paper towel.

❷ Meanwhile, combine the lamb and spices in a bowl and season with salt and pepper.

❸ Melt 1 tablespoon of the oil or fat in a large flameproof casserole dish over medium–high heat. Add the lamb in batches and seal until well browned, about 3 minutes per side. Remove from the dish and set aside. Reduce the heat to medium, melt the remaining oil or fat and add the onion. Cook, stirring occasionally, for 8 minutes until soft. Add the garlic and chilli and cook for 1 minute, then stir in the carrot and turnip.

❹ Return the lamb to the dish, add 1.25 litres of water and stir in the pomegranate molasses and bay leaves. Season with salt and pepper and bring to the boil.

❺ Reduce the heat to medium–low, cover and cook for 2 hours, skimming off the fat and adding more water if needed.

❻ Add the eggplant to the stew and cook for a further 30 minutes until the eggplant is soft and the meat is very tender.

❼ Scatter over the coriander and mint and serve with cauliflower rice.

PRESSURE COOKER Follow steps ❶–❷. Using your pressure cooker over medium heat, follow step ❸. Follow step ❹, but only add 850 ml of water rather than 1.25 litres. Close and lock the lid, then bring to high pressure and cook over medium heat for 20 minutes. Let the pressure drop naturally before opening the lid. Add the eggplant and cook, uncovered, over medium heat, stirring occasionally, for 30 minutes until tender. Follow step ❼.

SLOW COOKER Follow steps ❶–❹, but add only 850 ml of water rather than 1.25 litres. Transfer the ingredients from the dish to your slow cooker. Cover and cook on low for 8–10 hours until tender. Add the eggplant and cook, uncovered, on high for 45 minutes until tender. Follow step ❼.

The world's friendliest butcher Dominic O'Neill from GRUB (Grass Roots Urban Butchery) in Sydney cooked this recipe for me on my TV series, *The Paleo Way*. Dom is committed to working with the best farmers, who respect their animals, so that he can provide the best of the best to his customers – and that shows in the meat he supplies. The TV crew said this dish was their absolute favourite – and rightly so.

Lazy Man's LAMB SHOULDER

SERVES 6

2 tablespoons coconut oil or
 good-quality animal fat*
2 onions, finely chopped
2 garlic cloves, finely chopped
1–2 carrots, sliced
500 ml (2 cups) Beef Bone Broth
 (page 230)
1 × 400 g can whole peeled tomatoes
 (or 400 g tomatoes, diced)
sea salt and freshly ground
 black pepper
1 × 1.8 kg lamb shoulder
1½ teaspoons ground cumin

* See Glossary

❶ Heat the oil or fat in a large flameproof casserole dish over medium–high heat. Add the onion and cook, stirring occasionally, for 5–8 minutes until caramelised. Add the garlic and carrot and cook for 5 minutes until slightly softened and starting to colour. Pour in the broth and tomatoes and bring to the boil, then remove from the heat and season with salt and pepper.

❷ Preheat the oven to 90°C.

❸ Score the fat on the lamb using a sharp knife. Evenly rub the cumin and some salt and pepper into the fat.

❹ Place the lamb, fat-side up, in the dish and press down to submerge in the liquid.

❺ Cover the dish with a tight-fitting lid – or tightly seal with at least two layers of foil so no steam can escape. Transfer to the oven to braise for 10–12 hours. The lamb is ready when the meat pulls away easily from the bone. If there is any resistance, it needs to be cooked for a little longer.

PRESSURE COOKER Follow step ❶, using your pressure cooker over medium–high heat, but add only 350 ml of broth rather than 500 ml. Follow steps ❸–❹, close and lock the lid, then bring the cooker to high pressure and cook on medium heat for 1 hour. Let the pressure drop naturally before opening the lid.

SLOW COOKER Follow step ❶, but add only 350 ml of broth rather than 500 ml. Transfer everything from the casserole dish to your slow cooker. Follow steps ❸–❹, cover and cook on low for 12 hours until the lamb is very tender.

You simply can't go wrong with a delicious stew or casserole that has the flavours of Italy in it. Tomato, olives, rosemary, garlic and any type of meat on the bone slowly simmered in stock is a winner. The main thing dishes like this need is time, and a little love, to develop the flavour. As always, cook up heaps, so you have leftovers for breakfast or lunch the next day.

SERVES 6

Goat CASSEROLE

2 kg goat (or lamb) shoulder, cut into 8 cm pieces (ask your butcher to do this)

sea salt and freshly ground black pepper

3 tablespoons coconut oil or good-quality animal fat*

2 onions, chopped

8 garlic cloves, roughly crushed

1 leek, white part only, chopped

1 parsnip, chopped into 2 cm pieces

1 taro*, chopped into 2 cm pieces

2 bay leaves

1 teaspoon finely chopped thyme leaves

1 rosemary sprig, leaves picked and chopped

250 ml (1 cup) dry white wine

375 ml (1½ cups) Beef or Chicken Bone Broth (pages 230 and 234)

250 g cherry tomatoes, halved

12 pitted kalamata olives

1 handful of flat-leaf parsley leaves, roughly chopped

1 lemon, cut into 6 wedges

* See Glossary

❶ Preheat the oven to 160°C.

❷ Season the goat with a generous amount of salt and pepper.

❸ Melt the oil or fat in a large flameproof casserole dish over medium–high heat. Add the goat in batches and brown on each side for 1–2 minutes, then remove from the dish.

❹ Reduce the heat to medium, add the onion, garlic and leek and sauté for 5 minutes until the vegetables are soft and just starting to colour. Add the parsnip, taro, bay leaves, thyme and rosemary to the dish and stir well. Pour in the wine, bring to the boil and cook for 5 minutes until the liquid has reduced by half.

❺ Return the meat to the dish and pour in the broth.

❻ Cover with a lid and cook in the oven for 2½–3 hours until the meat is tender.

❼ Skim the fat off the casserole and reserve for another use, then add the cherry tomatoes and olives.

❽ Cover and return to the oven to cook for a further 30 minutes until the meat is falling off the bone.

❾ Season the casserole with salt and pepper if needed, sprinkle on the parsley and scatter over the lemon wedges.

PRESSURE COOKER Follow step ❷. Using your pressure cooker over medium–high heat, follow steps ❸–❹. Follow step ❺, but add only 250 ml of broth rather than 375 ml. close and lock the lid, then bring the cooker to high pressure and cook over medium heat for 30 minutes. Let the pressure drop naturally before opening the lid. Follow step ❼, then cook, uncovered, over medium heat for 15 minutes, stirring occasionally. Follow step ❾.

SLOW COOKER Follow steps ❷–❹, then transfer the ingredients from the dish to your slow cooker. Add the meat and 250 ml of broth, cover and cook on low for 8–10 hours until the meat is tender. Follow step ❼, then cook, covered, on low for 1 hour. Follow step ❾.

As you can tell from many of the recipes in this book, I love to use spices to elevate my dishes to new heights. And the craziest thing is it takes no longer to cook with spices than it does to cook without them. This wonderful stew is quite a spicy offering, using venison as the protein of choice. If you can't find venison, simply swap it for some good-quality grass-fed beef.

Chilli VENISON Stew

SERVES 4–6

1 kg boneless venison shoulder, cut into 2.5 cm pieces

sea salt and freshly ground black pepper

3 tablespoons coconut oil or good-quality animal fat*

2 onions, chopped

4 garlic cloves, finely chopped

1 tablespoon finely grated ginger

2 long red chillies, deseeded and chopped (leave the seeds in if you like it spicy)

1½ teaspoons ground cumin

1 teaspoon chipotle powder or smoked paprika

pinch of ground cinnamon

2 × 400 g cans whole peeled tomatoes, crushed (or 800 g tomatoes, diced)

400 ml Beef Bone Broth (page 230)

2 bay leaves

1–2 tablespoons chopped flat-leaf parsley leaves

Cauliflower Rice (page 233), to serve

* See Glossary

❶ Season the venison with salt and pepper.

❷ Melt the oil or fat in a large heavy-based saucepan over medium–high heat. Add the meat in batches and brown well on all sides, about 5 minutes. Set aside.

❸ Reduce the heat to medium, add the onion, garlic, ginger, chilli and spices to the pan and cook, stirring occasionally, for 5 minutes.

❹ Mix in the browned meat, tomatoes and broth, then add the bay leaves to the stew and season with salt and pepper.

❺ Bring the stew to the boil, reduce the heat to low and simmer, stirring occasionally, for 2½ hours until the meat is very tender.

❻ Sprinkle the parsley over the stew and serve with cauliflower rice or your favourite side.

PRESSURE COOKER Follow step ❶. Using your pressure cooker over medium–high heat, follow steps ❷–❸. Follow step ❹, but add only 280 ml of broth rather than 400 ml. Close the lid and lock it, then bring the cooker to high pressure and cook over medium heat for 30 minutes. Let the pressure drop naturally before opening the lid. Follow step ❻.

SLOW COOKER Follow steps ❶–❸, then transfer the ingredients in the saucepan to your slow cooker. Follow step ❹, but add only 280 ml of broth rather than 400 ml. Cover and cook on low for 8–10 hours until the meat is tender. Follow step ❻.

I adore this curry and its depth of flavour. And the added bonus of the meatballs popping out of the sauce makes it a firm family favourite. I encourage you to make bulk of this recipe, so that you have leftovers. Store in portions in the fridge to take to work or school for lunch, or freeze for those times you need to just grab and thaw something for a delicious meal when you get home from work.

SERVES 4

Lamb Kofta CURRY

600 g lamb mince

2 garlic cloves, finely chopped

1 tablespoon Turkish Spice Blend (page 244)

sea salt and freshly ground black pepper

2 tablespoons coconut oil

chilli flakes, to serve

1 small handful of mint and coriander leaves, chopped

Sauce

2 tablespoons coconut oil

1 onion, finely chopped

500 g cauliflower florets

3 garlic cloves, finely chopped

1 teaspoon ground cumin

1 teaspoon ground coriander

½ teaspoon paprika

½ teaspoon ground ginger

1 × 400 g can whole peeled tomatoes (or 400 g tomatoes, diced)

250 ml (1 cup) Beef or Chicken Bone Broth (pages 230 and 234)

1 × 400 ml can coconut cream

Salad

1 Lebanese cucumber, chopped

2 tomatoes, chopped

½ red onion, sliced

1 handful each of mint and flat-leaf parsley leaves, chopped

juice of 1 lemon, plus extra to serve

3 tablespoons extra-virgin olive oil

❶ Combine the lamb, garlic and Turkish spice blend in a bowl, mix well and season with salt and pepper. With wet hands, roll the lamb mixture into walnut-sized balls.

❷ Melt the oil in a large saucepan over medium heat. Add the meatballs in batches and seal until brown all over, 2–3 minutes. Remove from the pan and drain on paper towel.

❸ To make the sauce, melt the oil in the pan over medium heat, add the onion and sauté until soft and translucent, about 5 minutes. Stir in the cauliflower and cook for 2 minutes until starting to colour. Add the garlic and spices and cook for 30 seconds until fragrant, then mix in the tomatoes and broth and season with salt and pepper. Add the coconut cream, stir well and bring to the boil.

❹ Lower the heat and simmer the sauce for 20 minutes until reduced and thick.

❺ Gently stir the meatballs into the sauce and cook for 8 minutes until the meatballs are cooked through. Sprinkle over the chilli flakes and herbs and squeeze over some lemon juice if desired.

❻ Meanwhile, to make the salad, combine all the ingredients in a bowl and mix well. Season with salt and pepper and serve with the meatball curry.

PRESSURE COOKER Follow step ❶. Using your pressure cooker over medium–high heat, follow step ❷. Follow step ❸, but add only 125 ml of broth rather than 250 ml. Close and lock the lid, then bring the cooker to high pressure and cook over medium heat for 5 minutes. Let the pressure drop naturally before opening the lid. Follow step ❺ and cook, uncovered, for 8 minutes until the meatballs are cooked through. Follow step ❻.

SLOW COOKER Follow steps ❶–❹, but add only 125 ml of broth rather than 250 ml. Transfer the sauce and meatballs to your slow cooker. Cover and cook on low for 6 hours. Follow step ❻, scatter the chilli flakes and herbs over the curry and add a squeeze of lemon juice if desired.

This recipe was taught to me by Wendy Steward, who I met at one of my first paleo cooking classes. Growing up in Delhi and Bangalore, she ate this curry many times as a child. The original recipe is from a volume of cookbooks painstakingly hand-written in fountain pen by her maternal grandmother, Iris Flory, who was renowned for her amazing cooking. These cookbooks are family treasures and are still in Delhi – in Wendy's uncle's home.

SERVES 4

Brain CURRY

10 lamb brains

3 tablespoons coconut oil or
   good-quality animal fat*

3 green cardamom pods, crushed

2 whole cloves

2 large onions, chopped

sea salt

1–2 pinches of chilli powder

2 teaspoons finely grated ginger

3 garlic cloves, finely chopped

1 teaspoon desiccated coconut,
   finely ground (optional)

3 large tomatoes, chopped

250 ml (1 cup) Chicken Bone Broth
   (page 234), plus extra if needed

18 almonds, soaked in water for
   1 hour, drained

10 fresh okra pods*

2 silverbeet leaves, stalks removed,
   leaves roughly chopped (reserve
   the stalks for making broth)

Spice mix

3 teaspoons coriander seeds

1½ teaspoons poppy seeds

1½ teaspoons cumin seeds

¾ teaspoon garam masala

To serve

1 tablespoon coriander leaves

2 small green chillies, finely sliced

¾ teaspoon garam masala

See Glossary

❶ Wash the brains, then cut in half and soak in cold water for 15 minutes. Rinse well and pat dry.

❷ To make the spice mix, heat a large frying pan over medium–high heat. Add the coriander, poppy and cumin seeds and toast, tossing occasionally, for 1 minute until fragrant. Remove from the pan and grind to a fine powder using a mortar and pestle or a spice grinder. Mix in the garam masala and set aside.

❸ Heat the oil or fat in the pan over medium heat, add the cardamom and cloves and sauté for 30 seconds until fragrant. Add the onion and a pinch of salt and sauté, stirring occasionally, for 8 minutes until lightly caramelised and golden brown. Stir in the chilli powder, ginger, garlic and 1 tablespoon of water and cook for 30 seconds until softened. Add the spice mix and coconut (if using), stir and cook for 2 minutes until fragrant. Mix in the tomato and cook until the oil separates and comes to the surface, about 10 minutes.

❹ Pour the broth into the curry, then reduce the heat to low, mix in the almonds and add the brains, okra and silverbeet.

❺ Cook the curry for 8–10 minutes until the brains are cooked through and the okra is tender.

❻ Add more broth to the curry to thin the sauce if the curry is too dry. Serve with the coriander leaves and chilli, and a sprinkle of garam masala.

PRESSURE COOKER Follow steps ❶–❷. Follow step ❸, using your pressure cooker over medium heat. Close and lock the lid, then bring the cooker to high pressure and cook over medium heat for 5 minutes. Use the quick release method to open the lid (see page 11). Follow step ❹, close the lid and lock it, then bring the cooker to high pressure and cook for 5 minutes. Again, use the quick release method to open the lid. Follow step ❻.

SLOW COOKER Follow steps ❶–❷. Follow step ❸, then transfer everything in the frying pan to your slow cooker. Add the broth, almonds and brains, cover and cook on low for 1 hour and 35 minutes. Add the okra and silverbeet, cover and cook on low for 30 minutes. Follow step ❻.

Over the last decade lamb shanks have become expensive, so at home I use them in a celebratory meal. I have included the recipe for this delicious and mouth-watering lamb shank dish in this book, as I am sure you and your whole family will love this for a special lunch or dinner on a chilly weekend.

SERVES 6

Lamb Shank HARIRA

6 lamb shanks, French trimmed (ask your butcher to do this)
sea salt and freshly ground black pepper
2 tablespoons coconut oil
1 large onion, chopped
2 celery stalks, chopped
6 garlic cloves, finely chopped
1 teaspoon ground cumin
1 teaspoon ground turmeric
1 teaspoon ground cinnamon
½ teaspoon ground ginger
½ teaspoon freshly grated nutmeg
1 large pinch of saffron threads
1 × 400 g can diced tomatoes (or 400 g tomatoes, diced)
1 litre (4 cups) Beef or Chicken Bone Broth (pages 230 and 234) or vegetable stock
300 g sweet potato, diced
270 g kent pumpkin, diced
300 g zucchini, diced
400 g silverbeet or kale, stalks removed, leaves roughly chopped (reserve the stalks for making broth)
1 handful of coriander leaves, chopped
1 handful of flat-leaf parsley leaves, chopped
1 handful of mint leaves, chopped
2 lemons, cut into wedges (optional)

❶ Season the lamb shanks with salt and pepper. Melt the oil in a large saucepan over medium–high heat and add the shanks. Brown on all sides, about 6 minutes, then remove from the pan. Reduce the heat to medium and add the onion and celery and sauté, stirring occasionally, for 4–5 minutes until the vegetables are soft.

❷ Add the garlic and spices to the pan and sauté for 1–2 minutes. Stir in the tomatoes and cook for 3–4 minutes.

❸ Pour in the broth or stock, return the shanks to the pan and bring to the boil.

❹ Reduce the heat to medium–low and simmer the soup for 1½–2 hours.

❺ Add the sweet potato and pumpkin, season with salt and pepper and simmer for 10 minutes, then add the zucchini and silverbeet or kale.

❻ Simmer the soup for 10 minutes until all the vegetables are cooked and the meat is falling off the bone.

❼ Adjust the seasoning, stir in the coriander, parsley and mint and serve the harira with the lemon wedges, if desired. (If you would like the sauce to be a little thicker, simply remove the lamb shanks and keep warm, then simmer the sauce over medium heat until it reaches your desired consistency.)

PRESSURE COOKER Follow steps ❶–❷, using your pressure cooker over medium–high heat. Follow step ❸, but add only 700 ml of broth rather than 1 litre. Close the lid and lock it, then bring the cooker to high pressure over medium heat and cook for 45 minutes. Let the pressure drop naturally before opening the lid. Follow step ❺, close and lock the lid, then bring the cooker to high pressure and cook over medium heat for 5 minutes. Let the pressure drop naturally before opening the lid. Follow step ❼.

SLOW COOKER Follow steps ❶–❷. Transfer everything in the pan to your slow cooker. Follow step ❸, but add only 700 ml of broth rather than 1 litre. Cover and cook on low for 8 hours until the meat is tender. Follow step ❺ and cook, covered, on low for 2 hours or until tender. Follow step ❼.

Over the last 13 years I have had the pleasure to work with two amazing chefs, Monica and Jacinta Cannataci. Mon and Jac, who help me make these beautiful cookbooks, are from a Maltese background. When I told them I was doing a one pot book, they asked if they could include their favourite Maltese rabbit stew recipe. Of course, I couldn't be more proud to show off their heritage. Love you girls, and thanks for everything.

SERVES 4

Rabbit STEW

3 tablespoons coconut oil or good-quality animal fat*

1 rabbit (1–1.5 kg) with kidneys and liver, cut into 8 pieces (ask your butcher to do this)

400 g pork belly, skin on, cut into 2 cm pieces

2 onions, chopped

10 garlic cloves, chopped

3 carrots, cut into 2 cm cubes

2 tablespoons tomato paste

400 ml preservative-free red wine

4 thyme sprigs

2 bay leaves

500 g tomato passata

150 ml Chicken Bone Broth (page 234)

½ teaspoon mixed dried herbs

2 swedes or 2–3 parsnips, cut into 2 cm cubes

sea salt and freshly ground black pepper

1 handful of chopped flat-leaf parsley leaves

* See Glossary

❶ Preheat the oven to 150ºC.

❷ Melt 2 tablespoons of the oil or fat in a large flameproof casserole dish over medium–high heat. Add the rabbit pieces in batches and cook on each side for 2–3 minutes until golden brown, then remove from the dish. Add the pork belly and cook on each side for 2–3 minutes, then remove from the dish. Add the kidneys and liver to the dish and cook for 30 seconds on each side until golden. Remove from the dish and cool slightly before chopping into small pieces.

❸ Reduce the heat to medium, add the remaining oil or fat and the onion and cook for 5 minutes until translucent. Stir in the garlic, carrot and tomato paste and fry for 2 minutes until starting to colour. Add the wine, thyme and bay leaves, bring to the boil and cook for 5 minutes. Add the passata, broth, dried herbs and swede or parsnip, season with salt and pepper and stir well.

❹ Add the rabbit pieces and pork to the dish and bring to a simmer.

❺ Cover and bake for 2 hours until the rabbit is falling off the bone.

❻ Stir through the kidney and liver and finish with the chopped parsley.

PRESSURE COOKER Using your pressure cooker over medium–high heat, follow steps ❷–❹, then close and lock the lid. Bring to high pressure and cook over medium heat for 15 minutes. Let the pressure drop naturally before opening the lid. Follow step ❻.

SLOW COOKER Follow steps ❷–❹. Transfer all the ingredients from the casserole dish to your slow cooker. Cover and cook on low for 8 hours. Follow step ❻.

CHILINDRÓN MEATBALLS * *Oxtail stew*
* SAUSAGE AND VEGETABLE SOUP *
Beef mince curry * BEEF RENDANG
* *Indonesian beef ball soup with bone marrow* *
BEEF BOURGUIGNON * *Vietnamese beef curry*
* OXTAIL OSSO BUCO * *Bollito misto* *
OLD-SCHOOL MEATLOAF * *Standing rib roast
with aioli* * SPAGHETTI BOLOGNESE *
Spiced slow-roasted brisket

Chapter Six

BEEF

This meatball dish is inspired by the delicious Spanish chilindrón stew, which usually features onion, red capsicum and paprika. These meatballs are super easy and a great alternative to the classic Italian meatball. Enjoy with some fermented veg.

SERVES 4

Chilindrón MEATBALLS

3 tablespoons good-quality animal fat*

2 handfuls of baby spinach or kale leaves, chopped

2 garlic cloves, finely chopped

2 French shallots, finely chopped

500 g beef mince

150 g chicken livers, trimmed and finely chopped

2 tablespoons chopped flat-leaf parsley leaves, plus extra to serve

1 egg

½ teaspoon chilli flakes (optional)

sea salt and freshly ground black pepper

extra-virgin olive oil, to serve

Sauce

2 tablespoons good-quality animal fat*

1 large onion, chopped

4 garlic cloves, finely chopped

8 slices of prosciutto, finely chopped

2 tablespoons tomato paste

2 large red capsicums, chopped

1 × 400 g can whole peeled tomatoes, crushed (or 400 g tomatoes, diced)

2 bay leaves

1 teaspoon chopped thyme leaves

200 ml dry white wine

250 ml (1 cup) Chicken Bone Broth (page 234) or water

2 teaspoons paprika

2 pinches of chilli flakes (optional)

* See Glossary

❶ Melt 1 tablespoon of the fat in a large ovenproof frying pan over medium heat. Add the spinach or kale and cook until just wilted. Remove from the pan, squeeze out liquid, chop and set aside. Return the pan to medium heat and add another tablespoon of fat. Fry the garlic and shallot for 3 minutes until translucent. Set aside.

❷ Combine the mince, liver, spinach or kale, garlic, shallot, parsley, egg, chilli flakes (if using) and salt and pepper in a large bowl. Cover and place in the fridge for 30 minutes. Roll the mixture into golf ball–sized portions. Heat the remaining fat in the pan and fry the meatballs until golden on one side. Remove and set aside.

❸ For the sauce, melt the oil in the pan over medium heat. Add the onion and sauté for 5 minutes until translucent. Stir in the garlic, prosciutto and tomato paste and cook for 2 minutes. Add the capsicum, tomatoes, bay leaves and thyme.

❹ Cook, stirring occasionally, for 20 minutes until the tomatoes and capsicum have broken down to a thick sauce.

❺ Add the wine, broth, paprika and chilli flakes (if using) and bring to the boil.

❻ Reduce the heat to low and simmer for 30 minutes until slightly thickened.

❼ Season the sauce with salt and pepper and return the meatballs to the pan.

❽ Cook for 10 minutes until the meatballs are cooked through.

❾ Sprinkle on the extra parsley and drizzle over some olive oil to finish.

PRESSURE COOKER Using your pressure cooker over medium heat, follow steps ❶–❷. Follow step ❸, close and lock the lid, then bring to high pressure and cook over medium heat for 8 minutes. Let the pressure drop naturally before opening the lid. Follow step ❺, but add only 125 ml of broth rather than 250 ml. Close and lock the lid, bring to high pressure and cook over medium heat for 10 minutes. Use the quick release method to open the lid (see page 11). Follow steps ❼–❾.

SLOW COOKER Follow steps ❶–❺, but add only 125 ml of broth rather than 250 ml. Transfer the sauce to your slow cooker, follow step ❼, cover and cook on low for 6–8 hours. Follow step ❾.

I love to play around with classic dishes and, hoping for the best, add different spices and aromatics. This fusion dish, taking its inspiration from Vietnam and Italy, is the result of my recipe creating. Feel free to play around with it and try out other herbs, spices, proteins and vegetables.

SERVES 4–6

Oxtail STEW

1.4 kg oxtail, cut into 5 cm pieces (ask your butcher to do this)
sea salt and freshly ground black pepper
3 tablespoons good-quality animal fat*, plus extra if needed
1 onion, chopped
6 garlic cloves, chopped
1 tablespoon tomato paste
2 × 400 g cans whole peeled tomatoes, crushed (or 800 g tomatoes, diced)
250 ml (1 cup) preservative-free red wine
5 cm piece of ginger, finely grated
750 ml (3 cups) Beef or Chicken Bone Broth (pages 230 and 234)
2 lemongrass stalks, white part only, bruised with the back of a knife and cut into 3 pieces
1 celery stalk, cut into 5 cm lengths
2 carrots, halved lengthways and cut into 5 cm pieces
5 whole cloves
4 star anise
2 long red chillies, deseeded and roughly chopped

See Glossary

❶ Preheat the oven to 160°C.

❷ Season the oxtail pieces with salt and pepper.

❸ Heat 1 tablespoon of the fat in a roasting tin over medium–high heat. Add the oxtail pieces in batches and brown on all sides, about 6 minutes. Remove from the tin and set aside.

❹ Reduce the heat to medium and add the remaining fat to the tin if needed. Add the onion and cook for 5 minutes until translucent. Stir in the garlic and tomato paste and cook for 1 minute until the garlic is soft and fragrant.

❺ Add the tomatoes, wine, ginger and broth to the tin, stir and bring to the boil, then remove from the heat.

❻ Stir the lemongrass, celery, carrot, browned oxtail, cloves, star anise and chilli into the sauce.

❼ Tightly seal the tin with foil and transfer to the oven. Cook for 2½–3 hours, or until the oxtail is very tender and falling off the bone. Season with salt and pepper if needed and serve.

PRESSURE COOKER Follow step ❷. Using your pressure cooker over medium–high heat, follow steps ❸–❺, but add only 530 ml of broth rather than 750 ml. Follow step ❻, close and lock the lid, then bring the cooker to high pressure and cook over medium heat for 40 minutes. Let the pressure drop naturally before opening the lid. Season and serve.

SLOW COOKER Follow steps ❶–❺, but add only 530 ml of broth rather than 750 ml. Transfer all the ingredients from the roasting tin to your slow cooker. Follow step ❻, cover with the lid and cook on low for 8–10 hours. Season and serve.

Let's be honest – we all love a good snag, and what better way to make use of any you have leftover than turning them into a delicious soup? This is just like a meatball soup, but by using sausages, you can get the meal on the table a little more quickly. And it is a great recipe to get the kids into eating soup. The snags will entice them and the gut healing broth will go down a treat.

SAUSAGE and VEGETABLE Soup

SERVES 6

1 tablespoon coconut oil or good-quality animal fat*

6 paleo beef sausages

2 onions, chopped

2 slices of rindless bacon, chopped

3 garlic cloves, sliced

2 celery stalks, sliced

2 carrots, cut into 5 mm slices

1 turnip, cut into 1 cm cubes

3 litres Beef or Chicken Bone Broth (pages 230 and 234)

½ teaspoon ground turmeric

½ teaspoon ground cumin

2 zucchini, cut into 1 cm cubes

300 g pumpkin, cut into 2 cm pieces

2 large handfuls of silverbeet leaves, stalks removed, roughly chopped

sea salt and freshly ground black pepper

juice of 1 lemon

See Glossary

❶ Heat the oil or fat in a large saucepan over medium–high heat. Add the sausages and cook for 6 minutes, turning occasionally to brown all over. Remove from the pan and, when cool enough to handle, cut into 2 cm pieces.

❷ Reduce the heat to medium, add the onion and bacon to the pan and cook, stirring often, for 5 minutes until soft. Add the garlic, celery, carrot, turnip and sausage. Pour in the broth, stir in the turmeric and cumin and bring to the boil. Reduce the heat to medium–low, cover and simmer for 15 minutes.

❸ Add the zucchini and pumpkin to the pan and cook for a further 15 minutes, or until the zucchini and pumpkin are soft.

❹ Stir in the silverbeet and continue to cook for 5 minutes or until heated through.

❺ Season with salt and pepper and stir through the lemon juice. Ladle the soup into warmed bowls and serve.

PRESSURE COOKER Follow step ❶ using your pressure cooker. Place all of the ingredients except for the salt, pepper and lemon juice into the pressure cooker, close the lid and lock it. Bring the cooker to high pressure over medium heat and cook for 10 minutes. Naturally release the pressure before opening the lid. Follow step ❺.

SLOW COOKER Follow step ❶ using a large frying pan. Transfer all of the ingredients except for the salt, pepper and lemon juice to your slow cooker, cover and cook on low for 8 hours. Follow step ❺.

I love using mince at home, as it is quick, cheap and flavoursome. This is a delicious curry that you can have on the table in 30 minutes or so. My advice is to make triple the amount and, the next day, add some soft- or hard-boiled eggs to take to work or school for lunch.

SERVES 4–6

Beef Mince CURRY

2 tablespoons coconut oil

1 large onion, finely chopped

2 carrots, diced

2 tomatoes, chopped

1 long red chilli, deseeded and finely chopped

1 teaspoon black or brown mustard seeds

10 fresh curry leaves

4 garlic cloves, finely chopped

1½ tablespoons garam masala

2 teaspoons ground coriander

2 teaspoons ground cumin

½ teaspoon ground cardamom

½ teaspoon ground ginger

2 teaspoons ground turmeric

2 pinches of cayenne pepper (optional)

700 g beef mince

1 turnip, diced

1 × 400 ml can coconut cream

250 ml (1 cup) Beef or Chicken Bone Broth (pages 230 and 234)

juice of 1 lemon

sea salt and freshly ground black pepper

To serve

coriander leaves

lime wedges

Cauliflower Rice (page 233)

❶ Melt the oil in a wok or large frying pan over medium heat. Add the onion, carrot and tomato and cook, stirring occasionally, for 8 minutes until the vegetables are soft.

❷ Add the chilli to the pan and cook for 1 minute, then add the mustard seeds and cook for 15–20 seconds until they begin to pop. Stir in the curry leaves and garlic and sauté for 10 seconds, then add the dried spices and cook, stirring frequently, for 30 seconds until fragrant. Add the mince and cook, breaking up any lumps with a wooden spoon, for 5–6 minutes until browned. Stir in the turnip, coconut cream and broth and bring to the boil.

❸ Reduce the heat to low and simmer for 20 minutes until the sauce is slightly thickened and the beef and vegetables are cooked through.

❹ Mix in the lemon juice and season with salt and pepper. Scatter on the coriander leaves and serve with lime wedges and cauliflower rice.

PRESSURE COOKER Follow steps ❶–❷, using your pressure cooker over medium–high heat, but add only 170 ml of broth rather than 250 ml. Close the lid and lock it, then bring the cooker to high pressure over medium heat and cook for 10 minutes. Release the pressure before opening the lid. Follow step ❹.

SLOW COOKER Follow steps ❶–❷, but add only 170 ml of broth rather than 250 ml. Transfer everything in the pan to your slow cooker, cover and cook on high for 1½ hours. Follow step ❹.

Rendang is an Indonesian dish that dates back to the 1600s, so you could say it is a bit of a classic. The wonderful thing about rendang is the texture and flavour that develops during the stages of cooking. Serve it with cauliflower or broccoli rice or some Asian greens or salad, and some fermented vegetables like the traditional Indonesian achar.

SERVES 4–6

Beef RENDANG

2 tablespoons coconut oil
1.2 kg boneless beef short ribs,
    cut into 4 cm pieces
1 cinnamon stick
3 star anise
3 green cardamom pods
1 lemongrass stalk, white part only,
    cut into 10 cm lengths and bruised
4 kaffir lime leaves, torn
30 g (½ cup) toasted flaked coconut,
    plus extra to serve
1 tablespoon coconut sugar or honey
1 × 400 ml can coconut milk
2 teaspoons tamarind puree*
375 ml (1½ cups) Beef Bone Broth
    (page 230) or water
sea salt
lime wedges, to serve

Spice paste
4 French shallots, chopped
5 cm piece of galangal*, chopped
2.5 cm piece of fresh turmeric,
    chopped (or 1 teaspoon ground
    turmeric)
3 lemongrass stalks, white part
    only, chopped
5 garlic cloves, chopped
2.5 cm piece of ginger, chopped
8 dried red chillies, soaked in warm
    water and deseeded
3 whole cloves

* See Glossary

❶ Combine the spice paste ingredients and 2 tablespoons of water in the bowl of a food processor and whiz until very fine and smooth.

❷ Melt the oil in a large saucepan over medium–heat high, add the beef in batches and seal on all sides until brown, about 3 minutes. Remove from the pan and set aside.

❸ Add the cinnamon, star anise and cardamom to the pan and stir-fry over medium heat for 1 minute until aromatic. Add the spice paste and cook for a further minute.

❹ Return the beef to the pan, add the lemongrass and stir-fry for 1 minute.

❺ Stir the kaffir lime leaves, toasted coconut and coconut sugar or honey into the pan, then pour in the coconut milk, tamarind puree and broth.

❻ Reduce the heat to low and simmer, stirring occasionally, for 2½–3 hours until the beef is very tender.

❼ Season with a little salt and, if not sweet enough, add more coconut sugar or honey.

❽ Reduce the curry sauce, stirring frequently, until thick and sticky, about 15 minutes. Serve immediately with some extra coconut flakes scattered on top and lime wedges on the side.

PRESSURE COOKER Follow step ❶. Using your pressure cooker over medium–high heat, follow steps ❷–❺. Close and lock the lid, bring the cooker to high pressure and cook over medium heat for 30 minutes. Let the pressure drop naturally before opening the lid. Follow steps ❼–❽, cooking, uncovered and stirring occasionally, over medium heat.

SLOW COOKER Follow steps ❶–❹, then transfer the beef and spices in the saucepan to your slow cooker. Follow step ❺, cover and cook on low for 8 hours. Then, following steps ❼–❽, cook, uncovered, on high for 2 hours.

All the key elements of a paleo dish are included in this beautiful soup: good-quality bone broth, good fats, small amounts of animal protein and an abundance of colourful vegetables. The only thing missing is some fermented vegetables, which you can serve on the side. Try swapping the beef for prawn and fish, or pork and prawn, or just pork or chicken.

Indonesian BEEF BALL SOUP

SERVES 4   WITH BONE MARROW

1.3 litres Beef Bone Broth
   (page 230)
5 cm piece of ginger, cut into
   large pieces
2 cinnamon sticks
4 green cardamom pods, bruised
5 whole cloves
2 baby bok choy, trimmed
¼ baby Chinese cabbage (wong bok)
   (about 120 g), trimmed
1 bunch of broccolini (about 300 g)
700 g beef marrow bones, cut into
   5 cm pieces (ask your butcher to
   do this)
2 tablespoons fish sauce
3 tablespoons lime juice
sea salt and freshly ground
   black pepper
1 carrot, spiralised into thin
   noodles (or simply julienne
   with a knife)
chilli flakes, to serve (optional)

Beef balls

1 tablespoon coconut oil
¼ onion, finely chopped
2 garlic cloves, finely chopped
500 g beef mince
1½ tablespoons fish sauce
1 teaspoon sea salt
½ teaspoon freshly ground
   black pepper
½ teaspoon bicarbonate of soda
1 tablespoon finely grated ginger

❶ For the beef balls, melt the oil in a large saucepan over medium heat. Add the onion and cook for 3 minutes until soft, then add the garlic and cook for a further minute. Remove and set aside to cool. Place the remaining ingredients in a food processor, add the garlic and onion and 2 tablespoons of water and pulse until smooth. Transfer to a bowl, cover and refrigerate for at least 30 minutes.

❷ Pour the broth into the pan, add the ginger and spices and bring to the boil.

❸ Reduce the heat to medium–low and simmer the broth for 30 minutes.

❹ Meanwhile, blanch the bok choy, Chinese cabbage and broccolini separately in the simmering broth for 1–2 minutes, or until tender. Drain and set aside.

❺ Pop out the marrow from the bones, slice the marrow into 1 cm thick pieces and set aside. Reserve the bones for making broth.

❻ Working with 1 tablespoon of beef mixture at a time, roll into 3 cm balls.

❼ Remove the spices and ginger from the broth and discard. Drop in the beef balls and cook for 2 minutes, then add the bone marrow and cook for a further minute until the beef balls and bone marrow are cooked through. Gently stir in the fish sauce and lime juice and season with salt and pepper.

❽ Divide the beef balls, bone marrow, carrot and blanched vegetables between serving bowls. Ladle the broth over the top and sprinkle with chilli flakes, if desired.

PRESSURE COOKER Follow step ❶. Using your pressure cooker, follow step ❷, close and lock the lid, then bring to high pressure and cook over medium heat for 15 minutes. Let the pressure drop naturally before opening the lid. Reduce the heat to medium–low and follow step ❹. Then follow steps ❺–❽.

SLOW COOKER Follow step ❶. Using your slow cooker, follow step ❷, cover and cook on high for 2 hours. Add the bok choy, Chinese cabbage and broccolini, cover and cook for 10–15 minutes. Follow steps ❺–❻, remove the spices and ginger, then add the beef balls to the broth. Cover and cook for 15–20 minutes. Add the marrow and cook for a further few minutes. Stir in the fish sauce, lime juice, salt and pepper. Follow step ❽.

I am very proud to have started off learning traditional French cookery at culinary school, as it became the foundation for my technique and taught me to respect the produce I am working with. Beef bourguignon is a classic French dish that I think I learned to make in my very first semester. Here is my nod to those early days that helped shape the chef I am today. Bon appétit!

SERVES 4–6

Beef BOURGUIGNON

2 onions, finely chopped

2 large carrots, roughly chopped

6 garlic cloves, finely chopped

750 ml (3 cups) preservative-free red wine

400 ml Beef Bone Broth (page 230)

1.5 kg chuck steak, gravy beef, boneless short rib or beef cheek, fat trimmed and meat cut into 4 cm pieces

2 bay leaves

4 thyme sprigs

½ teaspoon freshly ground black pepper, plus extra for seasoning

sea salt

4 tablespoons coconut oil or good-quality animal fat*

3 tablespoons tapioca flour* (optional)

350 g speck, rind removed, flesh diced

5 French shallots, quartered

200 g button mushrooms, halved

* See Glossary

❶ Combine the onion, carrot, garlic, wine, broth, beef, bay leaves, thyme and pepper in a non-reactive dish. Cover with plastic wrap and refrigerate overnight.

❷ Remove the meat from the marinade and pat dry with paper towel. Season with salt and pepper and set aside.

❸ Strain the marinade through a fine sieve, reserving the liquid and the vegetables and herbs. Set aside.

❹ Melt 3 tablespoons of the oil or fat in a large flameproof casserole dish over medium–high heat. Add the meat in batches and cook for 2 minutes on each side until browned. Remove from the dish and set aside.

❺ Reduce the heat to medium, add the remaining oil or fat to the dish, then add the reserved vegetables and herbs and sauté for 6–8 minutes until starting to caramelise. Stir in the tapioca flour (if using) and cook for a further minute.

❻ Return the meat to the dish, pour in the reserved marinade and bring to the boil.

❼ Reduce the heat to low, cover and simmer for 1 hour until the meat is tender.

❽ Add the speck, shallot and mushrooms to the dish.

❾ Cook for a further 45 minutes until the shallot is very soft and the beef is meltingly tender. Season with salt and pepper and serve.

PRESSURE COOKER Follow steps ❶–❸. Follow step ❹, using your pressure cooker over high heat. Reduce the heat to medium–high and follow step ❺. Follow step ❻, but add only 300 ml of the marinade. Close and lock the lid, bring to high pressure and cook over medium heat for 30 minutes. Let the pressure drop naturally before opening the lid. Follow step ❽, close and lock the lid, bring to high pressure and cook over medium heat for 15 minutes. Let the pressure drop naturally before opening the lid. Season and serve.

SLOW COOKER Follow steps ❶–❺. Transfer everything in the dish to your slow cooker. Follow step ❻, but add only 300 ml of the marinade. Cover and cook on low for 8 hours. Follow step ❽, cover and cook on low for a further 2 hours.

Beef cheeks are very easy to prepare in one pot. All they need is a lot of time to cook so they become meltingly tender and some aromatics to infuse flavour. Here, I have teamed them with a lovely fragrant Vietnamese curry base to take them to a new level. If you can't find grass-fed beef cheeks, you can use beef tail or shin, chuck, lamb shanks, lamb osso buco or duck or chicken legs. Serve with a big bowl of salad or greens and fermented veg on the side.

SERVES 4–6

Vietnamese BEEF CURRY

1.2 kg beef cheeks, cut into
    2.5 cm cubes
3 tablespoons curry powder
2 teaspoons ground turmeric
pinch of cayenne pepper
1 tablespoon coconut sugar
    (optional)
sea salt and freshly ground
    black pepper
4 tablespoons coconut oil
4 red Asian shallots, cut into
    1 cm thick slices
1 carrot, chopped
4 cm piece of ginger, finely chopped
5 garlic cloves, sliced
650 ml Beef or Chicken Bone Broth
    (pages 230 and 234) or water
3 tablespoons fish sauce
300 ml coconut cream
1 large handful of water spinach*
    or spinach leaves
1 large handful of Vietnamese
    mint leaves
lime wedges, to serve

* See Glossary

❶ Preheat the oven to 160°C.

❷ Combine the beef cheeks, curry powder, turmeric, cayenne pepper and coconut sugar (if using) in a bowl and season with salt and pepper. Toss to combine, cover and marinate in the fridge for 15 minutes.

❸ Melt 2 tablespoons of the oil in a large flameproof casserole dish over medium–high heat. Add the shallot and carrot and cook for 4 minutes until slightly soft. Stir in the ginger and garlic and cook for 1 minute until the garlic starts to colour and is fragrant. Remove from the dish and set aside.

❹ Wipe the dish clean and melt the remaining oil over medium–high heat. Working in batches, add the marinated beef and cook for 5 minutes until well browned. Return all the meat and the garlic, shallot, carrot and ginger to the dish, pour in the broth and fish sauce and bring to a simmer.

❺ Cover the dish with the lid and transfer to the oven to cook for 2½ hours until the meat is tender. Stir in the coconut cream and cook, uncovered, on the stovetop over medium heat for a further 5 minutes.

❻ Season the curry with salt and pepper, if needed, and fold in the spinach. Scatter the Vietnamese mint leaves over the top and serve with the lime wedges on the side.

PRESSURE COOKER Follow step ❷. Using your pressure cooker over medium–high heat, follow steps ❸–❹, but add only 450 ml of broth or water rather than 650 ml. Close the lid and lock it, then bring the cooker to high pressure, reduce the heat to medium and cook for 40 minutes. Let the pressure drop naturally before opening the lid, then add the coconut cream, bring to a simmer and cook, uncovered, over medium–high heat for a further 5 minutes. Follow step ❻.

SLOW COOKER Follow step ❷. Follow steps ❸–❹, but add only 450 ml of broth or water rather than 650 ml. Transfer all the ingredients in the dish to your slow cooker. Cover and cook on low for 10–12 hours. Stir in the coconut cream, cover and cook for a further 30 minutes. Follow step ❻.

Is there a more comforting dish to make in the cooler months than this Italian classic? I have taken the liberty of using oxtail instead of shin bones for this variation, as oxtail is more affordable and I love its gelatinous nature and rich flavour. Great with a big bowl of green veg or salad and some fermented veg on the side.

SERVES 4–6

Oxtail OSSO BUCO

1.5 kg oxtail, cut into 5 cm pieces (ask your butcher to do this)
sea salt and freshly ground black pepper
4 tablespoons coconut oil or good-quality animal fat*
1 large onion, chopped
4 garlic cloves, sliced
2½ tablespoons paprika
2 tablespoons tomato paste
1 long red chilli, deseeded and finely chopped
½ celeriac (about 200 g), chopped into 2 cm pieces
250 g Swiss brown mushrooms, cut in half
150 ml preservative-free red wine
600 ml Beef Bone Broth (page 230)
1 × 400 g can diced tomatoes (or 400 g tomatoes, diced)
2 bay leaves
4 thyme sprigs
1 teaspoon finely grated lemon zest
1 handful of basil leaves, torn, to serve

* See Glossary

1 Preheat the oven to 160°C.

2 Season the oxtail with salt and pepper.

3 Melt the oil or fat in a large flameproof casserole dish over medium heat. Add the oxtail in batches and cook until well browned, 5–8 minutes. Remove from the dish and set aside.

4 Add the onion and sauté for 5 minutes until soft. Stir in the garlic and paprika and sauté for 1 minute until fragrant. Add the tomato paste, chilli and celeriac and cook for another minute, then return the oxtail to the dish and add the mushrooms.

5 Add the wine, broth, tomatoes, bay leaves, thyme and lemon zest and bring to the boil.

6 Remove the dish from the heat, cover with a lid or a few layers of foil and transfer to the oven. Cook for 2½–3 hours until the meat is tender and falling off the bone. Season with salt and pepper if needed.

7 Arrange the osso buco on a large platter or serve straight from the casserole dish. Scatter on the basil and serve.

PRESSURE COOKER Follow step **2**. Using your pressure cooker over medium–high heat, follow steps **3**–**5**, adding only 300 ml of broth rather than 600 ml. Close and lock the lid, then bring the cooker to high pressure and cook over medium heat for 45 minutes. Let the pressure drop naturally before opening the lid. Follow step **7**.

SLOW COOKER Follow steps **2**–**5**, adding only 300 ml of broth rather than 600 ml. Transfer all the ingredients from the casserole dish to your slow cooker, cover and cook on low for 8–10 hours. Follow step **7**.

Tip If you would like to thicken the sauce in this dish, simply mix 2 tablespoons of tapioca flour with a little water to form a paste, then stir it through the hot sauce at the end.

Bollito misto, an Italian dish of poached meats, is traditionally served for family gatherings. I encourage you all to try this, as you will have leftovers for days for lunches, salads and breakfasts, too. If you are an adventurous shopper, this is a great way to use different cuts of meat. I have included some staples here – like brisket, tongue and chicken – but you can also add pork belly, duck legs or whatever is affordable at your local butcher.

SERVES 6

Bollito MISTO

2 litres (8 cups) Chicken Bone Broth
    (page 234)
1 large red onion, cut into quarters
1 celery stalk, cut into 4 pieces
4 garlic cloves, peeled
3 flat-leaf parsley sprigs
1 rosemary sprig
3 bay leaves
sea salt and freshly ground
    black pepper
600 g beef brisket
1 beef tongue
4 chicken drumsticks
2 chicken breasts, skin on
10 Dutch carrots, leafy tops trimmed

Salsa verde
½ green capsicum, finely diced
1 French shallot, finely diced
2 garlic cloves, crushed
3 tablespoons baby capers
3 tablespoons finely diced gherkin
2 salted anchovy fillets
1 handful of flat-leaf parsley leaves,
    finely chopped
1 small handful each of mint and
    basil leaves, finely chopped
1 tablespoon finely chopped
    preserved lemon rind
2 tablespoons pine nuts, toasted
2 tablespoons finely chopped
    tarragon leaves
grated zest and juice of 1 lemon
125 ml (½ cup) extra-virgin olive oil

❶ Pour the broth into a saucepan large enough to hold the meat and vegetables. Add the onion, celery, garlic, parsley, rosemary and bay leaves and season with salt and pepper.

❷ Bring the broth to a simmer, add the brisket and gently simmer, skimming off any scum, for 1 hour. Add the tongue and continue to cook for 2½ hours.

❸ Add the chicken drumsticks to the broth and cook for 30 minutes, then add the chicken breasts and carrots and cook for 10 minutes until the chicken breasts are cooked through and the brisket and tongue are tender.

❹ To make the salsa verde, combine all the ingredients in a bowl and mix well. Add a little extra lemon juice if you prefer a sharper flavour and some more olive oil if the sauce is too thick. Set aside.

❺ Remove the meat, chicken and vegetables from the broth. Peel away the outer layer from the tongue and discard the skin. Cut the tongue into thick slices. Arrange the tongue, meat, chicken and vegetables on a large deep platter.

❻ Ladle some of the broth over the meat to keep it moist. (Keep the leftover broth for another use.) Serve with the salsa verde on the side.

PRESSURE COOKER Follow steps ❶–❷ using your pressure cooker. Add the chicken drumsticks, chicken breasts and carrots, close and lock the lid, bring the cooker to high pressure and cook over medium heat for 10 minutes. Let the pressure drop naturally before opening the lid. Follow steps ❹–❻.

SLOW COOKER Follow step ❶ using your slow cooker. Add the brisket and tongue, cover and cook on low for 9 hours. Add the chicken, cover and cook on low for 1 hour, then add the carrots, cover and cook for a further 40 minutes until the chicken is cooked through and the carrots are tender. Follow steps ❹–❻.

I love old-school favourites, and nothing is more old-school than a meatloaf filled with hard-boiled eggs. I love the humble meatloaf, as it is easy to make a lot so there are leftovers for the next day or two and it is equally delicious hot or cold. Serve with some fermented veg on the side and you are onto a winner.

SERVES 6–8

Old-school MEATLOAF

8 slices of rindless streaky bacon

800 g beef mince

4 tablespoons LSA* or almond meal

4 tablespoons Worcestershire sauce
  (for a recipe, see page 244)

1 tablespoon coconut oil or
  good-quality animal fat*

2 tablespoons chopped flat-leaf
  parsley leaves

1 carrot, finely diced

1 celery stalk, finely diced

150 g cabbage, finely shredded

1 onion, diced

2 garlic cloves, crushed

1 teaspoon caraway seeds, toasted

2 eggs, lightly whisked

1 tablespoon sea salt

2 teaspoons freshly ground
  black pepper

3 soft-boiled eggs, peeled

Glaze

4 tablespoons Tomato Ketchup
  (page 243)

1 tablespoon honey (optional)

1 tablespoon apple cider vinegar

* See Glossary

❶ Preheat the oven to 180°C.

❷ Line the base and sides of a 12 cm × 22 cm loaf tin with a piece of baking paper, cutting into the corners to fit and allowing the paper to extend 5 cm above the sides. Line the base and sides of the prepared tin with five slices of bacon, reserving the remaining slices for the top.

❸ Place the mince, LSA or almond meal, Worcestershire sauce, oil or fat, parsley, carrot, celery, cabbage, onion, garlic, caraway seeds, whisked eggs, salt and pepper in a bowl and mix until well combined.

❹ Pack half of the meat mixture firmly into the lined loaf tin and make three indentations for the eggs. Place the soft-boiled eggs in a single row, then cover with the remaining meat mixture and press down lightly to remove air bubbles, being careful not to break the eggs. Arrange the remaining slices of bacon lengthways over the top to completely cover, tucking them in so they don't overhang the sides. Bake in the oven for 25 minutes.

❺ Meanwhile, to make the glaze, mix the ketchup, honey (if using) and vinegar in a small bowl. Remove the meatloaf from the oven and baste the top with the glaze. Return the meatloaf to the oven and bake for a further 25 minutes, or until a meat thermometer inserted in the centre reaches at least 70°C.

❻ Allow the meatloaf to rest in a warm place for 10 minutes before turning out of the tin. Slice and serve with your favourite salad or roasted vegetables.

Rib roasts are not cheap, so this dish may not feature on your weekly dinner table, but it is perfect for when you have something to celebrate. The key here is to find a good-quality piece of grass fed and finished meat and do very little to it, except give it a kiss and caress with some wonderful spices.

Standing
SERVES 6–8
RIB ROAST WITH AIOLI

3 tablespoons good-quality animal fat*, melted
1 × 4.2 kg beef standing rib roast
450 ml olive oil
2 onions, sliced into 2 cm rings
4 rosemary sprigs
2 jalapeno chillies, deseeded
4 garlic cloves, unpeeled
2 egg yolks
½ teaspoon ground cumin
1 tablespoon finely chopped coriander leaves
3 tablespoons lime juice
1 teaspoon Dijon mustard
freshly ground black pepper

Rub
2½ tablespoons black peppercorns
2 tablespoons coriander seeds
1 tablespoon cumin seeds
1 cinnamon stick
6 whole cloves
2 tablespoons paprika
1 tablespoon smoked paprika
1 tablespoon ground allspice
1½ tablespoons sea salt

See Glossary

❶ To make the rub, combine the peppercorns, coriander seeds, cumin seeds, cinnamon and cloves in a frying pan over medium heat and toast, tossing and shaking the pan frequently, for 30 seconds until fragrant. Remove from the pan and cool completely. Grind to a fine powder using a mortar and pestle or a spice grinder. Mix in the paprika, smoked paprika, allspice and salt.

❷ Combine the fat and spice mix in a non-reactive dish, add the beef and evenly coat with the mixture. Marinate for 1 hour at room temperature.

❸ Preheat the oven to 190°C.

❹ Lightly drizzle some of the oil into a roasting tin and place a single layer of onion in the centre to form a bed for the roast. Scatter the rosemary on top and add the chillies and garlic — but keep these to one side, as they will be taken out halfway during cooking and used in the aioli.

❺ Place the beef on the onion and rosemary and roast in the oven for 30 minutes until the chillies are blistered and the garlic is soft. Remove the chillies and garlic and set aside. Return the beef to the oven and continue to roast for 1 hour until medium rare. Remove from the oven, loosely cover with foil and rest for 15 minutes.

❻ Meanwhile, to make the aioli, discard the stems and skin from the cooled chillies and garlic and place them in a blender. Add the egg yolks, cumin, coriander, lime juice and mustard and puree until smooth. With the motor running, slowly add the remaining oil in a steady stream and process until thick and emulsified. Season with salt and pepper.

❼ Carve the roast and serve with the aioli and your favourite side.

Bolognese is one of the most-cooked family meals in Australia and to be able to offer a paleo version is just brilliant. I serve it here with some vegetable noodles; however, you can bake a whole sweet potato until tender, then cut it open like a hotdog bun, fill the centre with bolognese and serve it with a delicious salad and some fermented veg on the side.

Spaghetti BOLOGNESE

SERVES 4

2 tablespoons coconut oil or good-quality animal fat*

1 onion, chopped

1 carrot, diced

1 celery stalk, finely diced

4 garlic cloves, finely chopped

500 g beef mince (or minced venison, kangaroo, lamb or emu)

2 tablespoons tomato paste

1 tablespoon chopped oregano leaves

200 ml dry, preservative-free red wine

500 g tomato passata or whole peeled tomatoes

300 ml Chicken Bone Broth (page 234)

pinch of chilli flakes (optional)

sea salt and freshly ground black pepper

baby basil leaves, to serve

Spaghetti

3 zucchini

2 carrots

* See Glossary

❶ To make the spaghetti, use the thick noodle blade on a spiraliser to create carrot and zucchini noodles. If you don't have a spiraliser, simply julienne the carrot and zucchini using a sharp knife. Set aside until needed.

❷ Melt the oil or fat in a large frying pan over medium–high heat. Add the onion, carrot and celery and cook for 4–5 minutes until the onion is soft. Stir in the garlic and cook for 1 minute until fragrant and starting to brown. Add the beef and brown, breaking up any lumps with a wooden spoon, for 5–6 minutes. Add the tomato paste, stir and cook for 1 minute. Mix in the oregano and wine and cook for 4–5 minutes until the wine has almost evaporated. Add the passata, half the broth and the chilli flakes (if using) and season with salt and pepper.

❸ Simmer on low heat for 30 minutes, adding more broth if needed.

❹ Bring a saucepan of salted water to the boil. Add the carrot noodles and cook for 30 seconds, then add the zucchini noodles and cook for a further 30 seconds until just tender. Drain well.

❺ Spoon the noodles into four serving bowls, top with the bolognese, then sprinkle on the basil.

PRESSURE COOKER Follow step ❶. Using your pressure cooker over medium heat, follow step ❷, but add only 100 ml of broth. Close the lid and lock it. Bring the cooker to high pressure and cook over medium heat for 15 minutes. Let the pressure drop naturally before opening the lid. Follow steps ❹–❺.

SLOW COOKER Follow step ❶. Follow step ❷, but add only 100 ml of broth. Transfer the ingredients from the pan to your slow cooker. Cover and cook on low for 8–10 hours. (Or cook on high for 4 hours.) Follow steps ❹–❺.

Tip I always add offal to my bolognese, burgers and meatballs to make them even more nutritious (I usually go with about 10 per cent of the total meat quantity – for this recipe it would be about 50 g of offal). Try using minced liver, heart, marrow or brain.

Whenever I think of the food scene in the United States, my mind goes to their amazing barbecue restaurants and food trucks, which have the most tantalising briskets. You don't need to leave your house to experience the taste. I guarantee the whole family will love this brisket served alongside a wonderful homemade slaw and fermented pickles or okra.

SPICED *Slow-roasted* BRISKET

SERVES 6–8

2 tablespoons coconut oil or
 good-quality animal fat*, melted
1 × 2 kg beef brisket
sea salt and freshly ground
 black pepper
4 French shallots, unpeeled, cut in
 half lengthways
1 garlic bulb, cut in half
 horizontally and broken into
 8 pieces
8 thyme sprigs
375 ml (1½ cups) Beef or Chicken
 Bone Broth (pages 230 and 234)

Spice rub
2 tablespoons smoked paprika
2 tablespoons paprika
1 tablespoon sea salt
2 teaspoons freshly ground
 black pepper
¼ teaspoon cayenne pepper
1 teaspoon ground turmeric

* See Glossary

① Preheat the oven to 180°C.

② Mix all the spice rub ingredients together in a small bowl and set aside.

③ Rub the oil or fat over the brisket, then lightly season with salt and pepper. Heat a large roasting tin over high heat, add the meat and seal on all sides for 3–4 minutes until browned, then remove from the tin and transfer, fat-side up, to a large plate. When cool enough to handle, evenly coat the sealed brisket with the spice rub.

④ Arrange the shallots, garlic and thyme in the tin in a single layer, then place the brisket on top and pour in the broth.

⑤ Place the tin in the oven and roast for 20 minutes until the spices brown. Reduce the temperature to 150°C. Cover the brisket firmly with a damp piece of baking paper and tightly cover the tin with a double layer of foil. Cook in the oven for 2 hours.

⑥ Check the brisket and add 125 ml of water if needed, then tightly reseal the tin and cook for another 2 hours until the brisket is tender.

⑦ Carve the meat and serve with your choice of roasted vegetables.

Chapter Seven
BASICS

BEEF BONE BROTH * *Beginners' kraut* * BROCCOLI RICE * *Cashew sour cream* * CAULIFLOWER RICE * *Chermoula* * CHICKEN BONE BROTH * *Chilli oil* * COCONUT YOGHURT * *Dukkah* * FERMENTED HOT CHILLI SAUCE * *Fish bone broth* * FISH BONE BROTH WITH KOMBU AND FENNEL * *Kimchi* * MACADAMIA MILK * *Mayonnaise* * PALEO HOISIN SAUCE * *Paleo sweet chilli sauce* * PICKLED CHINESE MUSTARD GREENS * *Spiced rice* * STRONG DASHI * *Thai red curry paste* * TOMATO KETCHUP * *Turkish spice blend* * WORCESTERSHIRE SAUCE * *Yellow curry paste* * ZUCCHINI RICE

BEEF BONE BROTH

about 2 kg beef knuckle and marrow bones
1 calf foot, chopped into pieces (optional)
3 tablespoons apple cider vinegar
1.5 kg meaty beef rib or neck bones

3 onions, roughly chopped
3 carrots, roughly chopped
3 celery stalks, roughly chopped
2 leeks, white part only, roughly chopped

3 thyme sprigs
2 bay leaves
1 teaspoon black peppercorns, crushed
1 garlic bulb, cut in half horizontally
2 large handfuls of flat-leaf parsley stalks

1 Place the knuckle and marrow bones and calf foot (if using) in a stockpot, add the vinegar and pour in 5 litres of cold water, or enough to cover. Set aside for 1 hour to help draw out the nutrients from the bones. Remove the bones from the water, reserving the water.

2 Preheat the oven to 180ºC.

3 Place the knuckle and marrow bones, calf foot (if using) and meaty bones in a few large roasting tins and roast in the oven for 30–40 minutes until well browned. Return all the bones to the pot and add the vegetables.

4 Pour the fat from the roasting tins into a saucepan, add 1 litre of the reserved water, place over high heat and bring to a simmer, stirring with a wooden spoon to loosen any coagulated juices. Add this liquid to the bones and vegetables.

5 If necessary, add the remaining reserved water to the pot to just cover the bones – the liquid should come no higher than 2 cm below the rim of the pot, as the volume will increase slightly during cooking.

6 Bring the broth to the boil, skimming off the scum that rises to the top. Reduce the heat to low and add the thyme, bay leaves, peppercorns and garlic. Simmer for 12–24 hours. Just before finishing, add the parsley and simmer for 10 minutes. Strain the broth into a large container, cover and place in the fridge overnight so that the fat rises to the top and congeals. Remove the fat and reserve for cooking; it will keep in the fridge for up to 1 week or in the freezer for up to 3 months.

7 The broth below the fat layer should be thick and gelatinous – the longer you cook the bones for, the more gelatinous it will become. Transfer the broth to smaller airtight containers and place in the fridge or, for long-term storage, the freezer. The broth can be stored in the fridge for 3–4 days or frozen for up to 3 months.

BEGINNERS' KRAUT

MAKES 1 × 1.5 LITRE JAR

400 g green cabbage
400 g red cabbage
1 beetroot, peeled
2 carrots (about 250 g in
    total)
1½ teaspoons sea salt

1 sachet vegetable
    starter culture*
    (this will weigh 2–5 g,
    depending on the
    brand)
See Glossary

1 You will need a 1.5 litre preserving jar with an airlock lid for this recipe. Wash the jar and all the utensils you will be using in very hot water. Alternatively, run them through a hot rinse cycle in the dishwasher.

2 Remove the outer leaves of the cabbages. Choose an unblemished leaf, wash it well and set aside.

3 Shred the cabbages, beetroot and carrot in a food processor or slice with a knife or mandoline, then transfer to a large glass or stainless steel bowl. Sprinkle the salt over the vegetables, mix well and cover with a plate.

4 Prepare the starter culture according to the directions on the packet. Add to the vegetables and mix thoroughly.

5 Using a large spoon, fill the prepared jar with the vegetable mixture, pressing down well to remove any air pockets and leaving 2 cm free at the top. The vegetables should be completely submerged in the liquid. Add more water, if necessary.

6 Take the clean cabbage leaf, fold it up and place it on top of the vegetables, then add a small glass weight (a shot glass is ideal) to keep everything submerged. Close the lid and wrap a tea towel around the jar to block out the light. Store in a dark place at 16–23ºC for 10–14 days. (You can place the jar in an esky to maintain a more consistent temperature.) Different vegetables have different culturing times and the warmer it is, the shorter the time needed. The longer you leave the jar, the higher the level of good bacteria present. It is up to you how long you leave it – some people prefer the tangier flavour that comes with extra fermenting time, while others prefer a milder flavour.

7 Chill before eating. Once opened, it will last for up to 2 months in the fridge when kept submerged in liquid. If unopened, it will keep for up to 9 months in the fridge.

BROCCOLI RICE

2 heads of broccoli
(about 800 g), roughly
chopped into florets
2 tablespoons coconut
oil or good-quality
animal fat*

sea salt and freshly
ground black pepper
* See Glossary

❶ Place the broccoli in the bowl of a food processor and pulse into tiny, fine pieces that look like rice.

❷ Heat the oil or fat in a large frying pan over medium heat, add the broccoli and cook, stirring occasionally, for 4–5 minutes until tender. Season with salt and pepper and serve with stews, stir-fries and curries.

CASHEW SOUR CREAM

155 g (1 cup) cashew nuts
juice of 1 lemon, plus
extra if desired
pinch of sea salt

❶ Soak the cashews in 750 ml of filtered water for 2–4 hours. Drain and rinse well.

❷ Place the cashews in the bowl of a food processor or in a high-speed blender, add the lemon juice, salt and 200 ml of filtered water and blend until smooth and creamy. Slowly pour in more water if needed and process to a sour cream consistency. Taste and add a little more lemon juice if you like your sour cream to be more tangy. Store in an airtight container in the fridge for up to 5 days.

CAULIFLOWER RICE

1 head of cauliflower (800 g–1 kg), roughly chopped

2 tablespoons coconut oil or good-quality animal fat*

sea salt and freshly ground black pepper

* *See Glossary*

❶ Place the cauliflower in the bowl of a food processor and pulse into tiny, fine pieces that look like rice.

❷ Heat the oil or fat in a large frying pan over medium heat, add the cauliflower and cook, stirring occasionally, for 4–5 minutes until softened. Season with salt and pepper and serve with stews, stir-fries and curries.

CHERMOULA

1 large handful of coriander leaves, chopped

1 large handful of flat-leaf parsley leaves, chopped

1 large handful of mint leaves, chopped

3 garlic cloves, chopped

2 teaspoons ground cumin

2 teaspoons ground coriander

1 teaspoon paprika

1 small red chilli, deseeded and chopped

3 tablespoons lemon juice

125 ml (½ cup) olive oil

sea salt and freshly ground black pepper

❶ Combine the herbs, garlic, spices, chilli and lemon juice in the bowl of a food processor.

❷ With the motor running, drizzle in the oil and process until smooth. Season with salt and pepper. The chermoula will last, stored in an airtight container, for 3–4 days in the fridge.

CHICKEN BONE BROTH

MAKES 3.5 LITRES

1–1.5 kg bony chicken parts (I like to use necks, backs, breastbones and wings)

2–4 chicken feet (optional)

2 tablespoons apple cider vinegar

1 large onion, roughly chopped

2 carrots, roughly chopped

3 celery stalks, roughly chopped

2 leeks, white part only, roughly chopped

1 garlic bulb, cut in half horizontally

1 tablespoon black peppercorns, lightly crushed

2 bay leaves

2 large handfuls of flat-leaf parsley stalks

❶ Place the chicken pieces in a stockpot, add 5 litres of cold water, the vinegar, onion, carrot, celery, leek, garlic, peppercorns and bay leaves and let stand for 1 hour to help draw out the nutrients from the bones.

❷ Place the pot over medium–high heat and bring to the boil, skimming off the scum that forms on the surface. Reduce the heat to low and simmer for 12–24 hours. The longer you cook the broth, the richer and more flavourful it will be. About 10 minutes before the broth is ready, add the parsley stalks.

❸ Strain the broth through a fine sieve into a large storage container, cover and place in the fridge overnight so that the fat rises to the top and congeals. Remove the fat and reserve for cooking; it will keep in the fridge for up to 1 week or in the freezer for up to 3 months.

❹ The broth below the fat layer should be thick and gelatinous – the longer you cook the bones for, the more gelatinous it will become. Transfer the broth to smaller airtight containers and place in the fridge or, for long-term storage, the freezer. The broth can be stored in the fridge for 3–4 days or frozen for up to 3 months.

CHILLI OIL

90 g (½ cup) chilli flakes, toasted

6 garlic cloves, crushed

500 ml (2 cups) olive oil

1 Combine the chilli flakes, garlic and oil in a saucepan over low heat. Heat the oil to 80°C and hold at this temperature for 10 minutes until the chilli and garlic are aromatic. Remove from the heat and cool to room temperature.

COCONUT YOGHURT

flesh and water of 4 young coconuts*

juice of 2 lemons or limes

1–2 vanilla pods, split and seeds scraped

maple syrup or honey, to taste

2 probiotic capsules*

* See Glossary

1 Combine the coconut flesh, one-third of the coconut water, the lemon or lime juice, vanilla seeds and maple syrup or honey in a blender and blend until smooth. Add more coconut water to thin, if desired.

2 Open your probiotic capsules, pour into the blender and give one final quick whiz. Pour into a 1 litre glass jar, cover with paper towel and allow to sit for 6–12 hours at room temperature so that the bacteria can proliferate (break down the yoghurt). The longer you leave it, the tangier the yoghurt will be. Store in the fridge in an airtight container for up to 2 weeks.

DUKKAH

MAKES 110 G

40 g (¼ cup) pine nuts
(activated if possible*)
4 tablespoons coriander
seeds
60 g white sesame seeds
¼ teaspoon ground
cumin

¼ teaspoon sea salt
pinch of chilli powder
¼ teaspoon baharat*
pinch of dried mint
* See Glossary

❶ Combine the pine nuts and coriander seeds in a large frying pan and toast over medium–high heat for 1 minute until the nuts start to colour. Add the sesame seeds and toast for another minute until golden brown.

❷ Pour the nut and seed mixture into the bowl of a food processor. Add the cumin, salt, chilli powder, baharat and mint and pulse to combine. Store in an airtight container in the pantry for 2–3 weeks.

FERMENTED HOT CHILLI SAUCE

MAKES 1 LITRE

1 sachet vegetable
starter culture*
(this will weigh 2–5 g,
depending on the
brand)

1.5 kg long red chillies
5 garlic cloves, peeled
2 tablespoons honey
2 teaspoons sea salt
* See Glossary

❶ You will need a 1.5 litre preserving jar with an airlock lid for this recipe. Wash the jar and utensils thoroughly in very hot water or run them through a hot rinse cycle in the dishwasher.

❷ Dissolve the starter culture in water according to the packet instructions (the amount of water will depend on the brand). Place the starter culture and all the remaining ingredients in the bowl of a food processor and process to a fine paste. Spoon into the preserving jar and close the lid to seal, leaving the airlock exposed, then wrap a tea towel around the jar to block out the light.

❸ Store in a dark place at 16–23ºC for 5–7 days. (You can place the jar in an esky to maintain a more consistent temperature.) After the chilli paste has bubbled and brewed for about a week, set a fine sieve over a bowl, tip the chilli paste into the sieve and press down with a wooden spoon to extract as much chilli sauce as possible. Pour the sauce from the bowl into a clean, sterilised 1 litre jar and close the lid to seal. Store in the refrigerator for several months..

FISH BONE BROTH

MAKES 3 LITRES

2 tablespoons coconut oil

2 celery sticks, roughly chopped

2 onions, roughly chopped

1 carrot, roughly chopped

125 ml (½ cup) dry white wine or vermouth (optional)

3 or 4 whole, non-oily fish carcasses (including heads), such as snapper, barramundi or kingfish

3 tablespoons apple cider vinegar

1 handful of thyme and flat-leaf parsley sprigs

1 bay leaf

❶ Melt the oil in a stockpot or large saucepan over medium–low heat. Add the vegetables and cook gently for 30–60 minutes until soft. Pour in the wine or vermouth (if using) and bring to the boil. Add the fish carcasses and cover with 3.5 litres of cold water. Stir in the vinegar and bring to the boil, skimming off the scum and any impurities as they rise to the top.

❷ Tie the herbs together with kitchen string and add to the saucepan. Reduce the heat to low, cover and simmer for at least 3 hours.

❸ Remove the fish carcasses with tongs or a slotted spoon and strain the liquid through a sieve into a large storage container. Cover and place in the fridge overnight so that the fat rises to the top and congeals. Remove the fat and transfer the broth to smaller airtight containers. The broth should be thick and gelatinous – the longer you cook the bones for, the more gelatinous it will become. Store in the fridge for 3–4 days or in the freezer for up to 3 months.

FISH BONE BROTH WITH KOMBU AND FENNEL

MAKES 2 LITRES

3 sheets dried kombu* (each 7.5 cm × 15 cm)

1 kg white-fleshed fish trimmings and bones, rinsed and scales removed (try snapper, barramundi or flathead)

2 large onions, quartered

1 fennel bulb, finely sliced

2 tablespoons chopped garlic

* See Glossary

❶ Cut small slits into the kombu with a pair of scissors to help release the flavour.

❷ Combine the kombu and 2.8 litres of water in a stockpot and set aside to soak until the kombu softens, about 2 hours.

❸ Add the fish trimmings and bones, onion, fennel and garlic to the pot, cover and bring to a simmer over medium–low heat. Simmer until the bones fall apart, about 1 hour. Remove the kombu and discard.

❹ Smash and press the solids in the pot with a large spoon to extract as much flavour as possible. Strain the broth through a fine sieve. If not using the broth immediately, cool at room temperature until lukewarm, about 30 minutes. Cover and refrigerate for 3–4 days. The broth can also be frozen for up to 3 months. .

KIMCHI

MAKES 1 × 1.5 LITRE JAR

½ Chinese cabbage
(wong bok) (about
500 g)
3 radishes or 1 daikon*
1 carrot
1 onion
1½ teaspoons sea salt
3–4 garlic cloves, finely
sliced
3 tablespoons grated
ginger

3–4 long red chillies,
deseeded and finely
sliced
2 large handfuls of
coriander roots, stalks
and leaves, finely
chopped
1 tablespoon Korean
chilli powder
(gochugaru)*
(optional)

1 teaspoon ground
turmeric (optional)
1 sachet vegetable
starter culture*
(this will weigh 2–5 g,
depending on the
brand)
* See Glossary

❶ You will need a 1.5 litre preserving jar with an airlock lid for this recipe. Wash the jar and utensils thoroughly in very hot water or run them through a hot rinse cycle in the dishwasher.

❷ Remove the outer leaves of the cabbage. Choose one, wash it well and set aside. Finely shred the cabbage, radishes or daikon, carrot and onion in a food processor. (You can also use a mandoline or knife to chop them finely.) In a large glass or stainless steel bowl, combine the cabbage with the radish or daikon, carrot and onion. Sprinkle on the salt and mix well. Add the garlic, ginger, chilli, coriander, chilli powder and turmeric (if using). Mix well, cover and set aside.

❸ Dissolve the starter culture in water according to the packet instructions (the amount of water will depend on the brand). Add to the vegetables and mix well. Fill the prepared jar with the vegetable mix, pressing down well with a large spoon or a potato masher to remove any air pockets. Leave 2 cm of room free at the top. The vegetables should be completely submerged in the liquid, so add more water if necessary.

❹ Fold up the clean cabbage leaf, place it on top of the mixture and add a small glass weight (a shot glass is ideal) to keep everything submerged. Close the lid, then wrap a tea towel around the jar to block out the light. Store in a dark place at 16–23°C for 10–14 days. (You can place the jar in an esky to maintain a more consistent temperature.) Different vegetables have different culturing times and the warmer it is, the shorter the time needed. The longer you leave the jar, the higher the level of good bacteria present and the tangier the flavour.

❺ Chill the kimchi before eating. Once opened, it will last for up to 2 months in the fridge when kept submerged in the liquid. If unopened, it will keep for up to 9 months in the fridge.

MACADAMIA MILK

MAKES 1 LITRE

160 g (1 cup) macadamia nuts

1 Place the macadamia nuts in a bowl, cover with 1 litre of filtered water and soak for 8 hours or overnight. Drain and rinse well. Place the nuts in a high-powered blender with 1 litre of filtered water and blend until smooth.

2 Line a bowl with a piece of muslin that is large enough to hang over the edge of the bowl (alternatively, you can use a nut milk bag). Pick up the edges of the muslin, bring together and twist to squeeze out all the milk. (The leftover solids can be used in place of almond meal when baking or making bliss balls.)

3 Pour the nut milk into a sterilised 1 litre bottle or jar and store in the fridge for up to 1 week. Shake the bottle before use as the milk will settle and separate over time.

MAYONNAISE

MAKES ABOUT 500 G

4 egg yolks
2 teaspoons Dijon
  mustard
1 tablespoon apple cider
  vinegar
1 tablespoon lemon juice
sea salt
400 ml olive oil or
  macadamia oil
freshly ground
  black pepper

1 Place the egg yolks, mustard, vinegar, lemon juice and a pinch of salt in the bowl of a food processor and process until combined. With the motor running, slowly pour in the oil in a thin stream and process until the mayonnaise is thick and creamy. Season with salt and pepper. (If you don't have a food processor, you can also use a hand-held blender for this recipe.) Store in a glass jar in the fridge for 4–5 days.

PALEO HOISIN SAUCE

MAKES ABOUT 160 ML

juice of 1 orange
2 tablespoons almond
   butter
1 teaspoon grated garlic
1 tablespoon grated
   ginger
2 teaspoons apple cider
   vinegar
2 teaspoons honey
4 tablespoons tamari or
   coconut aminos*

½ teaspoon Chinese
   five spice powder
1½ teaspoons sesame oil
½ teaspoon dried chilli
   flakes or powder
2 teaspoons tomato
   paste
2 tablespoons water
* See Glossary

1 Place all the ingredients in a saucepan and bring to
a simmer over medium–low heat. Cook for 5 minutes,
stirring constantly. Allow to cool.

2 Transfer the sauce to a blender and blend until
smooth. Store in a glass jar in the fridge for up to 2 weeks.

PALEO SWEET CHILLI SAUCE

MAKES ABOUT 350 G

125 ml (½ cup) coconut
   vinegar or apple cider
   vinegar
120 g honey
2 tablespoons fish sauce
3 garlic cloves
1 teaspoon finely grated
   ginger

2 long red chillies,
   chopped and most
   seeds removed
1½ tablespoons
   arrowroot*, mixed
   with 2 tablespoons
   water
* See Glossary

1 Place the coconut vinegar, honey, 100 ml of water,
the fish sauce, garlic cloves, ginger and chilli in the bowl
of a food processor and blend until fine.

2 Pour the mixture into a saucepan and bring to the
boil. Reduce the heat to low and simmer until the sauce
is reduced by half, about 10 minutes. Whisk in the
arrowroot paste and continue to whisk for 30 seconds
until thickened. Remove from the heat and cool. Store in
a glass jar in the refrigerator for up to 2 weeks.

PICKLED CHINESE MUSTARD GREENS

50 g sea salt
900 g small Chinese
   mustard greens (gai
   choy), left whole

2.5 cm piece of ginger,
   finely sliced
4 garlic cloves, grated
2 green serrano chillies,
   finely chopped

1 You will need a 2.5 litre preserving jar with an airlock lid for this recipe. Wash the jar and utensils thoroughly in very hot water or run them through a hot rinse cycle in the dishwasher.

2 To make the brine, dissolve the salt in 500 ml of water in a non-reactive container. Add the mustard greens, ginger, garlic and chilli to the jar, pressing down well with a large spoon to remove any air pockets and leaving 2 cm of room free at the top. Place a small glass weight (a shot glass is ideal) on top to keep the vegetables submerged in the brine.

3 Close the lid, leaving the airlock exposed, then wrap a tea towel around the jar to block out the light. Store in a dark place at 16–20°C for 3–4 weeks until the greens taste sour. (You can place the jar in an esky to maintain a more consistent temperature.)

4 Chill the mustard greens before eating. Refrigerate for up to 1 year unopened. Once opened, the greens will last for 9 months. The flavour of the greens becomes less intense and more nuanced as the greens age. I like them best after about 1 month.

SPICED RICE

1 small head of
   cauliflower (about
   600 g), florets and
   stalk roughly chopped
2 tablespoons coconut oil
1 teaspoon yellow or
   brown mustard seeds
2 teaspoons cumin seeds
2 cinnamon sticks
1 long red chilli, deseeded
   and finely sliced
1 onion, finely chopped
2 garlic cloves, finely
   chopped
2 teaspoons ground
   turmeric

pinch of cayenne pepper
   (optional)
80 g currants
125 ml (½ cup) Beef or
   Chicken Bone Broth
   (see pages 230 and
   234) or vegetable stock
   or water
sea salt and freshly
   ground black pepper
1 handful of almonds
   (activated if possible*),
   toasted (optional)
* *See Glossary*

1 Place the cauliflower in the bowl of a food processer and pulse until it resembles rice. Do not over-process as it will become mushy.

2 Melt the oil in a large frying pan over medium–high heat. Add the mustard seeds, cumin seeds, cinnamon and half the chilli and cook for 20 seconds until fragrant and lightly golden. Add the onion and garlic, then reduce the heat to medium and cook, stirring occasionally, for 5 minutes until the onion is translucent. Stir in the turmeric, cayenne pepper (if using) and currants and cook for a few seconds, then add the cauliflower rice and cook for 1 minute, tossing to coat. Pour in the broth, stock or water and cook, tossing occasionally, for 3–4 minutes until the cauliflower is tender and the liquid has evaporated. Season with a little salt and pepper and serve with the remaining chilli and the almonds if you like some crunch.

STRONG DASHI

MAKES 1 LITRE

4 sheets dried kombu*
(each 7.5 cm × 15 cm)

50 g (2 packed cups)
bonito flakes*

2 teaspoons sea salt

1½ teaspoons tamari or
coconut aminos*

See Glossary

1 Cut small slits in the kombu with a pair of scissors to help release the flavour. Place the kombu and 1.5 litres of water in a large saucepan and set aside to soak until the kombu starts to soften, about 2 hours.

2 Place the pan over medium heat and bring to a gentle simmer (ideally 60–71ºC), making sure that the water never boils. (Boiling the kombu gives the dashi an intense flavour and turns the broth cloudy. Cooking the kombu at a lower temperature yields a clearer broth.) Cook gently until the kombu is tender enough to be pierced easily with a chopstick and the broth has a mild sea-like aroma and a noticeable but delicate salty flavour, about 1 hour. Strain the broth, discarding the kombu.

3 Return the broth to the pan over medium–low heat until steam rises from the surface of the liquid (about 85ºC). Add the bonito flakes and salt and push down gently to submerge the flakes with a spoon. Do not stir, as you don't want to break up the fine pieces. Turn off the heat and let the bonito flakes steep in the hot broth for 5 minutes.

4 Strain the dashi through a fine sieve, taking care not to squeeze or press the flakes. Discard the bonito flakes. Season the dashi with the tamari or coconut aminos. If not using immediately, let the dashi cool at room temperature until lukewarm, about 30 minutes, then refrigerate, uncovered, until completely cool. Cover and refrigerate for up to 3 days or freeze for up to 3 months.

THAI RED CURRY PASTE

1½ tablespoons coriander seeds

1 tablespoon cumin seeds

1 teaspoon black peppercorns

12 dried long red chillies, deseeded and soaked in hot water for 15 minutes

4 tablespoons coconut oil

2–3 small red chillies, deseeded and chopped

2 tablespoons finely chopped red Asian shallot

2 tablespoons finely chopped garlic

1 tablespoon finely grated galangal*

2 tablespoons finely chopped lemongrass, white part only

1 tablespoon finely chopped coriander stalks

2 teaspoons shrimp paste

1 kaffir lime leaf, finely chopped

1 teaspoon sea salt

* See Glossary

❶ Combine the coriander seeds, cumin seeds and peppercorns in a frying pan and toast over medium heat for 2 minutes until fragrant. Remove from the pan and allow to cool. Grind to a fine powder using a spice grinder or a large mortar and pestle.

❷ Drain the water from the dried chillies and transfer the chillies to the bowl of a food processor. Add the dried spices and process to break down the chillies.

❸ Melt the coconut oil in the pan over medium heat. Add the small red chilli, shallot, garlic, galangal, lemongrass and coriander stalks and cook for 5 minutes until softened and fragrant. Combine with the ground spices and chilli in the food processor. Add the shrimp paste, lime leaf and salt and process to a fine smooth paste, adding up to 4 tablespoons of water to form a smooth paste. Store the paste in an airtight container in the fridge for up to 1 month.

TOMATO KETCHUP

180 g tomato paste

100 ml water (add more water if you prefer the sauce to be thinner)

1 tablespoon apple cider vinegar

1 teaspoon garlic powder

1 teaspoon onion powder

½ teaspoon ground cinnamon

¼ teaspoon freshly grated nutmeg

1 teaspoon honey

⅛ teaspoon ground cloves

❶ Mix the tomato paste and water in a small saucepan and place over a medium heat. Bring to a simmer, then remove from the heat and stir through the remaining ingredients until fully incorporated. Cool and store in an airtight glass jar or container in the fridge for 4 weeks.

TURKISH SPICE BLEND

MAKES ABOUT 100 G

35 g (⅓ cup) ground cumin

3 tablespoons dried mint

3 tablespoons dried oregano

2 tablespoons paprika

2 tablespoons freshly ground black pepper

2 teaspoons hot paprika

1 Combine all the ingredients in a bowl and mix well. Store in an airtight container in the pantry for up to 3 months.

WORCESTERSHIRE SAUCE

MAKES 150 ML

125 ml (½ cup) apple cider vinegar

2½ tablespoons coconut aminos* or tamari

½ teaspoon ground ginger

½ teaspoon mustard powder

½ teaspoon onion powder

½ teaspoon garlic powder

¼ teaspoon ground cinnamon

¼ teaspoon freshly ground black pepper

* See Glossary

1 Combine all the ingredients with 2 tablespoons of water in a saucepan and bring to the boil over medium heat, stirring occasionally. Reduce the heat to low and simmer for 10 minutes. Remove from the heat and allow to cool. Pour into a sterilised bottle and store in the fridge for up to 1 month.

YELLOW CURRY PASTE

6 dried long red chillies, soaked in hot water for 30 minutes
4 tablespoons coconut oil
10 garlic cloves, finely chopped
6 red Asian shallots, finely chopped
1 teaspoon shrimp paste
5 cm piece of ginger, grated
2.5 cm piece of galangal*, grated
5 cm piece of fresh turmeric, grated (or 2 tablespoons ground turmeric)
4 kaffir lime leaves, chopped
1 teaspoon sea salt
* See Glossary

❶ Drain the chillies, reserving 4 tablespoons of the soaking liquid.

❷ Melt the oil in a frying pan over medium heat. Add the chillies and the remaining ingredients and cook, stirring occasionally, for 5–10 minutes until softened and fragrant.

❸ Transfer the chilli mixture to the bowl of a food processor, add the reserved soaking liquid and blend to a smooth paste. Store in a sealed container in the refrigerator for up to 1 month.

ZUCCHINI RICE

2 large zucchini (about 500 g)
1 teaspoon coconut oil
sea salt (optional)

❶ Slice off the ends of the zucchini and discard. Julienne the zucchini with a mandoline or julienne peeler, spiralise into noodles with a spiraliser, or simply slice them with a sharp knife into long, thin strips.

❷ Place the zucchini noodles or strips on a chopping board and cut into tiny pieces the size of rice grains.

❸ Heat the oil in a wok or frying pan over medium heat. Add the zucchini rice and sauté for 5 minutes until softened. Season with salt, if desired.

GLOSSARY

ACTIVATED NUTS AND SEEDS

Nuts and seeds are a great source of healthy fats, but they contain phytic acid, which binds to minerals such as iron, zinc, calcium, potassium and magnesium so that they can't be readily absorbed. Activating nuts and seeds lessens the phytates, making sure that we absorb as many of the good things as possible. Activated nuts and seeds are available from health food stores. Or to save money and make your own, simply soak the nuts or seeds in filtered water (hard nuts, like almonds, need to soak for 12 hours; softer nuts, like cashews and macadamias, only need 4–6 hours). Rinse well under running water, then spread out on a baking tray and place in a 50°C oven or dehydrator to dry out. This will take anywhere from 6 to 24 hours, depending on the temperature and the kind of nuts or seeds you are using. Store in an airtight container in the pantry for up to 3 months.

ARROWROOT

Arrowroot is a starch made from the roots of several tropical plants. In Australia, arrowroot and tapioca flour are considered the same, even though they are actually from different plants. It can be found at health food stores and some supermarkets. *See also* Tapioca Flour.

BAHARAT

Baharat is a Middle Eastern spice blend that includes black pepper, coriander, paprika, cardamom, nutmeg, cumin, cloves and cinnamon. It is great for seasoning meats and vegetables, adding to dips and sauces, or using as a dry rub or marinade for veggies, meat and fish. Look for baharat at Middle Eastern grocers and delis.

BITTER MELON

Bitter melon, also called bitter gourd, is a member of the gourd family. The cucumber-shaped fruit has soft, uneven skin with irregular lengthways ridges and, as its name suggests, a bitter flavour. Bitter melon is great in stews, soups, stir-fries and curries. It can be found in some large supermarkets and Asian grocers, and is best when firm and brightly coloured.

BONITO FLAKES

Bonito flakes are made from the bonito fish, which is like a small tuna. The fish is smoked, fermented, dried and shaved, and the end product looks similar to wood shavings. Bonito flakes are used to garnish Japanese dishes, to make sauces such as ponzu and soups such as miso, and to make the Japanese stock dashi. You can find bonito flakes in Asian food stores.

CASSIA BARK

Cassia bark is a type of cinnamon that originates from southern China and is cultivated throughout South East Asia. Cassia is the most common type of cinnamon found on supermarket shelves and varies from Ceylon or 'true' cinnamon in a number of ways. Quills from cassia bark are thick and not easily broken, while Ceylon cinnamon sticks have thin, fibrous layers. Cassia also has a stronger and spicier taste. Both cassia and Ceylon cinnamon have been used medicinally for thousands of years to treat colds, arthritis, high blood pressure and abdominal pain.

COCONUT AMINOS

Coconut aminos is made from the raw sap of the coconut tree, which is naturally aged and blended with sea salt. It is a great alternative to soy sauce as it has a higher amino acid content and no gluten. It is also slightly less salty than tamari. You'll find coconut aminos in health food stores.

DAIKON

Daikon, or Japanese radish, is a large, white radish that is commonly used in Japanese, Korean and South East Asian cuisines. It has a wide variety of uses – it is pickled, grated into sauces, simmered in broths and even stir-fried. Daikon is low in calories and contains high levels of vitamin C. It can be found at Asian grocers and some supermarkets.

GALANGAL

Galangal is similar in appearance to ginger and has been used in Thai cooking for more than a thousand years. It is available in Asian supermarkets and some regular supermarkets, and is believed to relieve indigestion, flatulence, nausea and hiccups. It is fantastic in many kinds of Asian dishes, especially curries.

GOOD-QUALITY ANIMAL FAT

I use either coconut oil or good-quality animal fats for cooking as they have high smoke points (meaning they do not oxidise at high temperatures). Some of my favourite animal fats to use are lard (pork fat), tallow (rendered beef fat), rendered chicken fat and duck fat. These may be hard to find – ask at your local butcher or meat supplier, or look online for meat suppliers who sell them.

KELP NOODLES

Kelp noodles are clear noodles made from seaweed. They contain more than 70 nutrients and minerals, including iron, potassium, magnesium, calcium and iodine, and more than 20 amino acids. Kelp noodles are great for stir-fries, casseroles, soups and salads. You can find them at health food stores.

KOMBU

Kombu is a high-protein sea vegetable, rich in calcium, iron, iodine and dietary fibre. It is salty and savoury and plays a vital role in Japanese cuisine. Kombu can be used in a similar way to bay leaves – add a few pieces to a stew or curry for a flavour boost and remove them after cooking. Kombu can be found in Asian grocers and is mainly sold dried or pickled in vinegar. Dried kombu is often covered with a white powder from natural salts and starch. It is harmless and can be easily removed with a damp cloth.

KOREAN CHILLI POWDER (GOCHUGARU)

Korean chilli powder is made from thin red chillies that are dried in the sun and ground. It has smoky, fruity sweet notes with a hot kick, and is used to make classic Korean dishes such as kimchi and bulgogi. It is also great for stir-fries, dipping sauces and meat marinades. You can find Korean chilli powder in Asian supermarkets.

LSA

LSA stands for linseed, sunflower seed and almond meal. It can be added to smoothies, sprinkled on salads and fruit and added to just about any meal for a protein and vitamin boost. It is high in fibre, essential fatty acids, B vitamins, magnesium and calcium. LSA should be stored in the fridge as it is high in unsaturated fats, which can go rancid. You can buy LSA from health food stores or supermarkets.

OKRA

Also known as ladyfingers, okra is popular in many cuisines, including Indian, Israeli, Japanese and Mediterranean. It is best used when very young, while the pod is green, tender and immature. Okra is a good source of vitamin A and C, fibre, calcium and iron. It has a glutinous texture when cooked and gives body to soups, stews and curries.

POMEGRANATE MOLASSES

Pomegranate molasses is a beautifully thick, tangy and glossy reduction of pomegranate juice that has a sweet and sour flavour and is rich in antioxidants. It is used in Middle Eastern countries for glazing meat and chicken before roasting, and in sauces, salad dressings and marinades. Pomegranate molasses is available from Middle Eastern grocers and some delis.

PROBIOTIC CAPSULES

Probiotic capsules contain live bacteria that can help to regulate digestion, clear up yeast infections and assist with conditions such as irritable bowel syndrome. They need to be kept in the fridge. The capsules can be swallowed whole, or opened up and used to ferment drinks such as kefir. Probiotic capsules can be found at pharmacies and health food stores.

PSYLLIUM HUSKS

Psyllium, also known as ispaghula, is a gluten-free, light-brown soluble fibre produced from the *Plantago ovata* plant, native to India and Pakistan. Psyllium is an indigestible dietary fibre that is primarily used to maintain intestinal health, as the high fibre content absorbs excess liquid in the gut. When exposed to liquids, the husks swell up to create a gel. It is therefore important to drink plenty of fluids when consuming psyllium. Psyllium products can be found at health food stores and some supermarkets.

SAMPHIRE

Samphire, often called asparagus of the sea, is a native succulent that comes in two types: rock and march.

Only the march variety, also known as glasswort, is widely available. The plants are vibrantly green with a woody base and many small branches. Samphire has a distinctive crisp and salty taste that pairs well with most seafood. It can also be used in pesto, salads and salsa verde and as a garnish. Samphire grows freely in Australia, but state regulations vary, so inquire before foraging. Samphire is rich is vitamin A, calcium and iron, and contains phytochemicals that protect the body from disease. It is available for purchase online.

SUMAC

Sumac is a spice made from red sumac berries that have been dried and crushed. It has antimicrobial properties and a tangy, lemony flavour that makes it ideal for pairing with seafood. It's also delicious in salad dressings.

TAMARIND PUREE

Tamarind is a sticky, sour fruit that grows in brown pods on the tamarind tree, which is native to Africa. To make tamarind puree, or paste, the fruit must be separated from the pods and seeds. The puree is used as a souring agent, particularly in Indian dishes, chutneys and curries. It is also used as an ingredient in sauces and side dishes for pork, chicken and fish. It can be found at Asian grocers and some supermarkets.

TAPIOCA FLOUR

Tapioca flour is made by grinding up the dried root of the manioc (also known as cassava) plant. It can be used to thicken dishes or in gluten-free baking. You can find tapioca flour at health food stores and some supermarkets. *See also* Arrowroot.

TARO

Taro is a potato-like, gluten-free root vegetable popular in large parts of Asia, the Pacific, West Africa and South America. Taro flesh is white or pink and sometimes turns purple when cooked. It has a sweet, nutty flavour with a similar texture to potato and can be used in both sweet and savoury dishes. Taro is toxic raw so must either be cooked or soaked in water overnight before eating. It can be found at selected greengrocers and Asian markets.

VEGETABLE STARTER CULTURE

A vegetable starter culture is a preparation used to kickstart the fermentation process when culturing vegetables. I prefer to use a broad-spectrum starter sourced from organic vegetables rather than one grown from dairy sources, as this ensures your fermented product will contain the highest number of living, active bacteria and will produce consistently successful results free of pathogens. Vegetable starter culture usually comes in sachets and can be purchased at health food stores or online.

WATER SPINACH

Also known as Chinese watercress, water spinach has high levels of protein, calcium, iron, potassium and vitamins A, B and C. Water spinach can be used in almost anything, including stir-fries, quiches, omelettes, soups, fillings, casseroles and curries. You can find it at Asian grocers and some fruit and vegetable markets.

WOOD EAR FUNGUS

Wood ear fungus, which is sometimes called cloud ear, black fungus or tree ear, is a high-protein, low-calorie mushroom. Wood ear has a grey-brown to black colour and a rubbery texture. It's popular in Asian cooking and can be added to soups, stir-fries and salads. Wood ear is sold fresh in Asian grocers but is more commonly found in a dried form that needs to be reconstituted before eating.

YOUNG COCONUTS

Young coconuts are harvested at around 5–7 months and are usually white in colour. The best way to open one is to cut a circle in the top using a large knife and then prise this circle off. The amount of coconut water inside varies, but is usually around 250 ml. It is a good source of potassium and makes a refreshing drink on a hot day. Once you've poured the water out of the coconut, you can scoop out the soft flesh using a spoon. Look for young coconuts at Asian food stores and health food stores.

THANK YOU

Endless gratitude to my exquisite partner in life and love, Nicola. It is an honour to share this journey with you! Thank you for nurturing Chilli, Indii, Shikoba, Orlando and me with your unconditional love and guidance and all of your deliciously nourishing food. I love you, Angel!

To my bunnies, Indii and Chilli — you know this book wouldn't have come about if it weren't for the two of you. I love you both so much and you are both so unique in your own special ways. I hope that by the time your own children are at school this way of living will be considered normal and the current dietary guidelines considered extreme.

To Mark Roper (photography) and Deb Kaloper (styling) — thanks for once again making my food shine brightly!

To Steve Brown (photography) and Lucy Tweed (styling) — thanks for the extra lifestyle images for the book and the brilliant cover shots.

To Mary Small and Jane Winning — once again, it was a pleasure working with you to create another much-needed book.

To Megan Johnston — thank you for your careful and thorough editing.

To Jacqui and Dan at Northwood Green — thank you for creating such a gorgeous design for the book.

To Monica and Jacinta Cannataci — girls, I can't thank you enough, and I am so happy that you have discovered that food really is medicine. You are the doctors of the future.

To Charlotte Ree — thanks for being the best publicist any author could wish to work with.

To Mum — thanks for passing on your love of cooking.

And finally to my mentors and the trailblazers in health and nutrition, I couldn't have done it without you: Nora Gedgaudas and Lisa Collins, Dr Libby, Trevor Hendy, Luke Hines, Helen Padarin, Pete Melov, Rudy Eckhardt, Pete Bablis, William (Bill) Davis, Tim Noakes, Gary Fettke, David Perlmutter, Gary Taubes, Frank Lipman, Wes and Charlotte Carr, Nahko Bear, Michael Franti, Trevor Hall, David Gillespie, Ben Balzer, Loren Cordain, Bruce Fife, Mat Lalonde, Martha Herbert, Joseph Mercola, Sally Fallon, Dr Natasha Campbell-McBride, Kitsa Yanniotis and Donna Gates.

INDEX

A PLUM BOOK

First published in 2016 by
Pan Macmillan Australia Pty Limited
Level 25, 1 Market Street,
Sydney, NSW 2000, Australia

Level 1, 15–19 Claremont Street,
South Yarra, Victoria 3141, Australia

Design by Dan Peterson and Jacqui Porter, Northwood Green
Photography by Mark Roper (with additional photography by Steve Brown)
Prop and food styling by Deb Kaloper (with additional styling by Lucy Tweed)
Edited by Megan Johnston
Typeset by Pauline Haas
Index by Jo Rudd
Colour reproduction by Splitting Image Colour Studio
Printed and bound in China by 1010 Printing International Limited

A CIP catalogue record for this book is available from the National Library
of Australia.

The publisher would like to thank Chasseur (www.chasseur.com.au) for
generously supplying props for the book.